IMAGES
of America

HAMPTON ROADS
THE WORLD WAR II YEARS

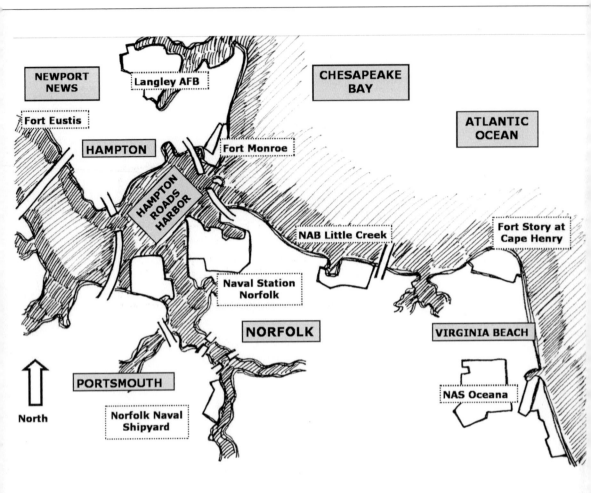

NEWPORT NEWS

Langley AFB

CHESAPEAKE BAY

Fort Eustis

ATLANTIC OCEAN

HAMPTON

Fort Monroe

HAMPTON ROADS HARBOR

NAB Little Creek

Fort Story at Cape Henry

Naval Station Norfolk

NORFOLK

VIRGINIA BEACH

North

PORTSMOUTH

NAS Oceana

Norfolk Naval Shipyard

HAMPTON ROADS, VIRGINIA. The Gateway to Southeastern Virginia, Hampton Roads (also known as Tidewater) includes 16 municipalities; the region contains such cities as Chesapeake, Hampton, Newport News, Norfolk, Portsmouth, Suffolk, Virginia Beach, and Williamsburg. It is a metropolitan area with a combined population of more than 1.5 million. The original name, Southampton Roadstead, was given in the 1600s for the royal governor, who was formerly of Southampton, England. The nautical term "roadstead" means "safe anchorage," referring to the myriad of harbors, rivers, bays, and inlets in the region. It was the water that gave life to the region, and made it attractive for the military, particularly the Navy. There has been some military presence in Hampton Roads for almost 400 years, since the establishment of the Jamestown Fort by the first colonists. By World War II, there were almost 400 military bases, offices, schools, depots, annexes, air stations, auxiliary air fields, departments, ports, and shipyards in the region, representing every branch of the service. Today, the region has the largest naval concentration in the world. (PEH.)

IMAGES
of America

HAMPTON ROADS
THE WORLD WAR II YEARS

Patrick Evans-Hylton

ARCADIA

Copyright © 2005 by Patrick Evans-Hylton
ISBN 0-7385-1766-6

Published by Arcadia Publishing
Charleston SC, Chicago IL, Portsmouth NH, San Francisco CA

Printed in Great Britain

Library of Congress Catalog Card Number: 2004114465

For all general information contact Arcadia Publishing at:
Telephone 843-853-2070
Fax 843-853-0044
E-mail sales@arcadiapublishing.com
For customer service and orders:
Toll-Free 1-888-313-2665

Visit us on the internet at http://www.arcadiapublishing.com

NAVAL AIR STATION NORFOLK—MAY 13, 1941. This aerial view shows the air station on the eve of World War II. By this date, it was evident that the United States would eventually be pulled into the war. The next week, on May 21, President Roosevelt declared an unlimited state of national emergency. Hampton Roads was ready to step to the plate and serve patriotically. (HRNM.)

CONTENTS

Acknowledgments   6

Introduction   7

1.   The Military History of Hampton Roads   9

2.   Planning for War   17

3.   Military Bases and Presence   25

4.   On the Home Front   63

5.   V-E Day, V-J Day, and the War's Aftermath   107

6.   Hampton Roads Military: Postwar Through Today   115

7.   How to Contact   121

About the Author   128

Bibliography   128

ACKNOWLEDGMENTS

Compiling information and photographs that chronicle Hampton Roads, Virginia, during the World War II years was no small task. It was only possible because of the assistance and expertise of many giving and gifted individuals. To everyone who lent their time, talent, and support in this effort, I thank you.

I would like to personally thank the following individuals who went above and beyond in their assistance and support: Kathryn Korfonta and Katie White of Arcadia Publishing; Fielding Tyler and Julie Pouliot of the Old Coast Guard Station Museum; Joe Judge of the Hampton Roads Naval Museum; Peggy Haile McPhillips of the Norfolk Public Library; Al Chewning, author of *The Approaching Storm: German U-Boats off the Virginia Coast During World War II*; Troy Snead of Naval Air Station Oceana; Megan Steele of the Virginia Air & Space Center; and Dave Parker, author of *History Next Door: Stories of World War II by Hampton Roads Veterans*.

Thank you, also, to Debby Padgett of the Jamestown-Yorktown Foundation; Dinah Everett of the Isle of Wight County Museum; Carl Warren Weidenburner; and Sarah Sager of Newport News/Williamsburg International Airport.

Special thanks for moral support and encouragement is due to my friends and my family, especially Wayne.

INTRODUCTION

Since the English established their first permanent settlement in the New World, there has been a military presence in what is today known as Hampton Roads.

On April 26, 1607, after a little more than four months of being at sea, 104 men and boys eyed the shores of Virginia. The ships dropped anchor at Cape Henry, and the settlers came ashore.

George Percy, one of the explorers, wrote: "The nine and twentieth day we set up a cross at Chesupioc Bay, and named the place Cape Henry." They then sailed on, into the Chesapeake Bay and up what is now the James River, looking for a site suitable for settlement. Present-day Jamestown is that place.

The colonists built a fort in June 1607 to protect against attacks from Indians and Spaniards and thus began the first incident of homeland security on what is now American soil.

Virginia would grow and lead the way with other colonies to form the United States. Along the way, there would be battles at home and abroad. Forts and bases would be built. Men would join all branches of the military service to defend the state and the nation.

The region had a military history dating back more than 300 years when the nation headed toward a second world war in the 1930s. As the United States watched the military aggression of Germany and Japan, by mid-decade, the government turned face from its isolationist policies and began strengthening defenses. By 1938, land was being purchased to expand the Norfolk Naval Air Station, part of a $4 million construction program. Employment again soared at the shipyard; by the summer of 1940, it added on average 1,000 new workers each month. The population in the region swelled with all the newcomers.

The vital role the area would play was underscored on July 29, 1940, when President Franklin D. Roosevelt came to Norfolk to tour the naval base and shipyard. He watched the construction of new maritime craft and the expansion of the air station. "A year from now we are going to be a lot safer," Roosevelt said, encouraged by the signs of progress.

Even before the Japanese attack on Pearl Harbor on December 7, 1941, Hampton Roads was in a full-fledged defense boom. Housing was at a premium; in Norfolk, the vacancy rate on dwellings dropped to around three percent in 1940. In fact, some beds were rented in shifts. The construction of emergency housing couldn't keep up with the need. Neither could transportation—streetcars were filled to capacity with the new military and civilians that came to town. Food and other necessities were in short supply, too.

After the official start of the war (Congress passed a joint resolution declaring war on Japan on December 8, 1941; German and Italy declared war on the United States three days later), things only got tighter.

Folks in Hampton Roads rationed food and gasoline. Citizens were asked to turn in scrap metal (Norfolk city council made it a misdemeanor to throw away a tin can in 1943), wood, rubber, and even cooking grease.

It was patriotic to grow a Victory Garden and put away your own food for the coming months, as well as volunteer at the Red Cross, the United Service Organization (USO), or with the civil defense. It was every American's duty to buy war bonds and give blood.

Air raids and blackouts were common occurrences, as was the presence of the enemy just off the coast. Beginning in 1942, around a dozen German U-boats plied the waters of the Atlantic, firing torpedoes at anything they could—military, commercial, or civilian. Oil, fuel, and wreckage often washed ashore at Virginia Beach.

The Hampton Roads Port of Embarkation was reactivated on June 15, 1942, in Newport News and was the portal that sent almost a million troops and more than 12 million tons of cargo on more than 3,000 ships overseas in little over 3 years.

Major offenses, such as Operation Torch, the successful invasion of North Africa, were planned and practiced here.

And then it was over. On May 7, 1945, Germany surrendered and May 8 was declared V-E (Victory in Europe) Day. In August, atomic bombs were dropped over the Japanese cities of Hiroshima and Nagasaki, forcing the Japanese to surrender; V-J (Victory in Japan) Day was celebrated on August 14.

Many of the soldiers, sailors, and civil defense workers stationed in Hampton Roads returned home; others stayed. The momentum of the military buildup in the region remained, however. At the end of the war, Norfolk Naval Base and Air Station remained the largest military installation in the world. Today, Hampton Roads has the largest concentration of naval operations anywhere.

PHOTOGRAPH LEGEND:

AJC: From the personal collection of Al Chewing.
FT: From the personal collection of Fielding Tyler.
HRNM: From the archives of the Hampton Roads Naval Museum.
NASO: From the archives of Naval Air Station Oceana.
NNWI: From the archives of Newport News/Williamsburg International Airport.
NPL: From the archives of Norfolk Public Library.
OCGS: From the archives of the Old Coast Guard Station Museum.
VASC: From the archives of the Virginia Air & Space Center.
PEH: From the personal collection of Patrick Evans-Hylton
All other photographs individually credited.

One

THE MILITARY HISTORY OF HAMPTON ROADS

From the establishment of Jamestown Fort in 1607 to the concentration of some 200,000 active duty military personnel and their family members in Southeastern Virginia, the military history of Hampton Roads is long and varied. The region has been a part of every conflict in the country's 400-year history.

The American Revolution would end on the battlefield in Yorktown with the British surrender of General Lord Cornwallis on October 19, 1781. Naval maritime history would be set with the Civil War battle between the Monitor and Merrimac in Hampton Roads Harbor, March 8–9, 1862.

Thousands would leave to fight World War I through the Hampton Roads Port of Embarkation in Newport News, and more than a million would in World War II. Hampton Roads would again send her sons and daughters to fight in Korea, in Vietnam, in the first Gulf War, and today, in the War on Terror.

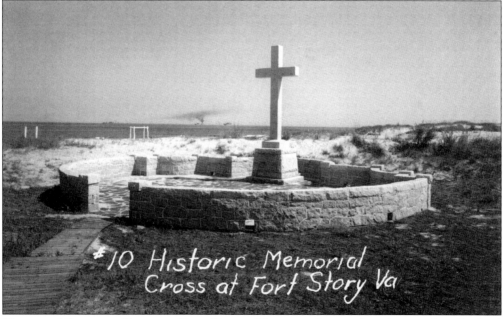

HISTORIC MEMORIAL CROSS AT FORT STORY, VIRGINIA. It was a long journey from England to the New World, and the sight of land was a welcome one. This granite cross, erected by the National Society of the Daughters of the American Colonists in 1935, commemorates the first landing of English settlers in 1607. The ships would continue on, and the colonists would establish Jamestown and construct the Jamestown Fort. (OCGS.)

JAMESTOWN FORT: THE FIRST ENGLISH SETTLEMENT. This mid-20th century painting by Richmond, Virginia artist Julien Binford depicts the building of the Jamestown Fort. One hundred and four men and boys landed at James Island on May 12, 1607; by June 15, they had constructed their first fort to protect against Native Americans and the Spanish. (Jamestown-Yorktown Foundation.)

WATCHING GUARD. The historical interpreters in this photo at Jamestown Settlement depict the job of watching guard at Jamestown Fort. Settlers, under the direction of Capt. John Smith, each had their own task, including those who acted as militia. Protecting the homeland was paramount, but so was growing the colony: "For in Virginia, a plaine Souldier that can use a Pick-axe and spade, is better than five Knights," said Smith. (Jamestown-Yorktown Foundation.)

You Say You Want a Revolution.
After Britain imposed a series of taxes on
the American colonies starting in 1764,
seeds of discontent were sown. Patriots, such
as these interpreters at the Yorktown
Victory Center, formed the Continental
Army, and the American Revolution, with
a goal of autonomy from England, began in
1775 and ended in 1781. George
Washington, a Virginian, became the
nation's first president in 1789. (Jamestown-
Yorktown Foundation.)

"The Meeting of Washington and Lafayette at Yorktown, 19th October 1781."
That is the title of this c. 1890 painting by Georges-Jules-Auguste Cain. Virginia's rich military
history became richer with the surrender of the British at Yorktown, following a three-week
siege by American and Allied (French) forces, ensuring American independence. Today,
Jamestown and Yorktown are popular tourist destinations. For more information, visit
www.historyisfun.org. (Jamestown-Yorktown Foundation.)

DEFENDER OF NORFOLK AND PORTSMOUTH. The frigate USS *Constellation* was built in 1797 and patrolled the area surrounding Hampton Roads during the War of 1812, breaking a blockade by the British and harboring at Fort Norfolk, which is now open to the public. Visit *www.norfolkhistorical.org/fort* for more information. This photo shows the ship in Portsmouth in June 1914. The ship was rebuilt in 1854, has since been refurbished, and is open for tours in Baltimore, Maryland. (Naval Historical Center.)

BATTLE OF THE IRONCLADS. One of the Civil War's most famous battles took place in Hampton Roads Harbor as the USS *Monitor* and the *Merrimac* (CSS *Virginia*) squared off and battled March 8–9, 1862, after the *Merrimac* terrorized Union ships and sunk the sloop *Cumberland*. Thousands lined the shores to watch the two iron-fortified ships fight. It ended in a stalemate. (Library of Congress.)

DECK AND TURRET OF USS MONITOR. This July 9, 1862 photo shows officers on the deck of the *Monitor* as it floats down the James River. The ironclad is part of naval history, and the battle with the *Merrimac* showed the world wooden warships would forever be obsolete. Today, the Mariners' Museum is restoring elements recovered from the sunken ship. For more information, visit *www.monitorcenter.org.* (Library of Congress.)

RAISING KEEL. This 1875 photo shows maritime construction at Norfolk Naval Ship Yard (NNSY), which is actually in Portsmouth. It, along with Newport News Shipbuilding (NNS), has produced hundreds of military, commercial, and civilian ships and other vessels for use worldwide. NNSY began as the Gosport Shipyard in 1767; NNS delivered its first ship in 1891. The ironclad *Merrimac* was converted at Gosport in 1861. (HRNM.)

REMEMBER THE MAINE. This June 1907 stern view of the USS *Maine* shows the ship at Point Comfort; the homeport was Norfolk. The destruction of the ship in Havana Harbor (Cuba) in 1898, killing 260 aboard, was a catalyst in leading the country into the Spanish-American War. Although reported at the time that an enemy mine sunk the ship, it is now known that a munitions accident aboard caused the tragedy. (Naval Historical Center.)

Birds Eye View of the Exposition.

BIRD'S EYE VIEW OF THE EXPOSITION. This 1907 postcard shows the Jamestown Exposition at the Sewell's Point area of Norfolk. The expo was held to celebrate the 300th anniversary of the founding of Jamestown. On this site in 1917, the United States Naval Operating Base and Training Station (now Norfolk Naval Base) was established; 1,400 sailors from St. Helena Training Station in Berkley marched to the new base. (OCGS.)

COPYRIGHT ENRIQUE MULLER.   U. S. S. "PORPOISE" AND "SHARK."   COPYRIGHT 1907 BY JAMESTOWN A. & V. CO.

RUB-A-DUB-DUB, A BUNCH OF MEN AND TWO SUBS. This 1907 Jamestown Exposition postcard of the USS *Porpoise* and *Shark* submarines reads on the back: "This view presents an excellent example of the latest invention in the way of infernal machines used in naval warfare." Norfolk was on its way to being a navy town. By 1917, Norfolk led the nation in navy recruiting in proportion to population. (OCGS.)

THE WAR TO END ALL WARS. Located at Twenty-fifth Street and West Avenue in Newport News, the Victory Arch, built in 1919, greeted returning World War I troops as they disembarked from ships at the nearby docks. Today, the arch and its eternal flame serve as a memorial for all the armed forces. The arch's inscription reads, "Greetings with love to those who return; a triumph with tears to those who sleep." (PEH.)

INTO THE WILD BLUE YONDER. Pictured here is the USS *Langley*, c. 1923, launching a DT-2. Built as the *Jupiter*, it was converted into the first United States aircraft carrier at the Norfolk Naval Ship Yard; tests aboard set naval and aviation history. In 1910, Eugene Ely was the first to fly from the deck of a cruiser, also in Norfolk, launching a Curtiss biplane from the deck of the cruiser *Birmingham*. (VASC.)

IT'S FUN TO STAY AT THE YMCA. The Naval YMCA in this early 20th-century photo is testament to the growing number of military—navy in particular—in Norfolk and Hampton Roads. By World War II, there were almost 400 military bases, offices, schools, depots, annexes, air stations, auxiliary air fields, departments, ports, and shipyards in the region, representing every branch of the service. (HRNM.)

Two

PLANNING FOR WAR

The War to End All Wars had been over for little more than a decade when the seeds of another global conflict were sown with the Japanese invasion of Manchuria in 1931. Throughout the 1930s, a number of acts of aggression by Japan, Germany, and Italy occurred. By 1939, there appeared to be no diplomatic solutions to the mounting discord, and on September 3, Britain and France declared war on Germany, starting World War II.

America remained largely neutral, but there was no doubt where the country's sympathies lay: "This nation will remain a neutral nation, but I cannot ask that every American remain neutral in thought as well," said President Roosevelt.

Although the United States entered the war following the Japanese attack on Pearl Harbor in December 1941, the U.S. Navy was already fighting an undeclared war on German U-boats, which had been sinking military, commercial, and civilian ships in the Atlantic for a year or more.

Planning for war in Hampton Roads meant the buildup of military bases in the region; by 1938, the army established a large supply depot at Sewell's Point and the navy started a significant expansion at the Norfolk Operating Base.

Many joined the service, either by volunteering or through conscription, which was established in 1940. On the home front, folks hunkered down, rationed precious supplies needed for the effort, and readied themselves for the fight ahead.

WAR ON THEIR MINDS. Americans had watched the buildup to war for years before the attack on Pearl Harbor in 1941. Japan invaded China in 1937, Germany invaded Austria in 1938, and the conflict kept growing. When war completely broke out in 1939, it was evident the United States could no longer remain neutral. Here, recruits sign up at a Norfolk Coast Guard enlistment office and plan to go to war. (OCGS.)

CHECKING THE DRAFT NUMBERS IN NORFOLK, OCTOBER 23, 1940. The first peacetime conscription took place with the Selective Training and Service Act of 1940. After the United States entered World War II, a new selective service act made men between 18 and 45 liable for military service and required all men between 18 and 65 to register. Between 1940 and 1947, more than 10 million men had been inducted. (NPL.)

SIGNING UP, BUILDING UP. Clyde McCoy and his band enlist in the navy in this early 1940s photo. As war momentum grew, so did the number of people and bases. Norfolk Naval Operating Base grew more than 1,500 acres in 1940–1941, land was acquired for a section base at Little Creek, Oceana Naval Air Station was carved from a farm in Virginia Beach, and military and civil workers alike flooded into town. (NPL.)

MANLY YES, BUT I WANT TO HELP, TOO. Everyone wanted to show their patriotism. Many women took civilian jobs, and others joined auxiliary military branch units, like this woman enlisting in the Women's Army Auxiliary Corps (WAACS) (later Women Army Corps [WACS]). Others included Women's Auxiliary Air Forces (WAAFS), Women's Auxiliary Ferrying Squadron (WAFS), Women's Air Force Service Pilots (WASPS), and SPARS (women coast guard members, from the motto *Semper Paratus*, which means "always ready"). (NPL.)

REMEMBERING PEARL HARBOR BY ENLISTING, DECEMBER 16, 1941. Ron Spangler of Norfolk signed up like the fellow in this photo following the attack. In Dave Parker's book *History Next Door*, a collection of stories from Hampton Roads veterans, Spangler is quoted as having said, "He was only 17 years old, but he knew that when he fought the Japanese he wanted to do it as a Marine . . . 'I wanted to fight for my country. Patriotism, I guess.' " (NPL.)

OCEAN LINERS PASSING VIRGINIA BEACH. VA.

ON THE WATERFRONT. As America moved toward war, folks realized how vulnerable they may have been on the home front. Because of the large concentration of military and civilian contractors, as well as their strategic location at the mouth of the Chesapeake Bay, locals and newcomers alike took action to ensure their safety. A blackout was imposed on municipalities in the region, like Norfolk and Virginia Beach. Volunteers looked for enemy aircraft. Convoys escorted commercial ships along the coast and into the Chesapeake Bay and Hampton Roads Harbor. Folks practiced air raids at work, home, and at play. Netting was strung between Cape Henry and Cape Charles in an effort to prevent German U-boats from cruising into the region (or up to the Potomac River and into Washington, D.C.). As the war loomed, tensions did, too. (Above: FT; Below: OCGS.)

PROTECTING THE COAST. Protection of Hampton Roads and all of the Virginia coastline came from the wide assortment of military bases in the region, such as Fort Story, as shown in this January 1941 image. The photo shows three-inch guns on line, possibly the 71st Coastal Artillery, 1st Battalion. Note the coast guard station in the background, which no longer stands. (FT.)

UNITED STATES COAST ARTILLERY—NORFOLK, VIRGINIA. This postcard from the U.S. Army Signal Corps shows some of the unit's activities employed to keep the coast safe as tensions with Germany and Japan built. The Signal Corps pioneered the development of radar to detect approaching aircraft as well as mobile communications and deciphering machines. (OCGS.)

HOLD THE PRESSES. Jack Scratch, the dog, and the staff of the *Virginian-Pilot* newspaper are pictured here the evening of December 7, 1941. When the attack on Pearl Harbor occurred, around 2:00 p.m. Eastern Time, a lone copy boy was on duty (and subsequently overwhelmed with phone calls.) But when they heard, newsmen headed into the office to get the story. A special edition hit the streets by 6:00. (NPL.)

A COLD SUNDAY. On December 7, 1941, winter was in the air, and the *Virginian-Pilot* headline was: "Roosevelt Sends Personal Plea to Mikado, Direct Action Seen Last Move To Avert Open Break; Tokyo Is Now Mobilizing Vast Army." By midday, news of the Japanese attack on Pearl Harbor came, and by evening, these Japanese Americans were rounded up as the nation went to war. (NPL.)

ROUND-UP OF JAPANESE AMERICANS. Within an hour of the announcement of the Japanese attack on Pearl Harbor on December 7, 1941, persons of Japanese descent were rounded up in Norfolk and surrounding communities. Naval Intelligence, which had long kept a list of Japanese in the area (approximately 40), broadcasted their names and addresses to local police for pickup. It was a similar scene across the country. Later, under Executive Order 9066 signed by President Roosevelt on February 19, 1942, interment camps, or War Relocation Centers, were established to hold not only Japanese Americans, but German Americans and Italian Americans, as well as their respective nationals, even those who were married to native or naturalized U.S. citizens. The U.S. Supreme Court argued that the internment camps were legal and justified for military and security reasons. The last of the camps was closed in March 1946. (NPL.)

HITLER BEWARE! That's the message on the shell, written by the crew of solders from Battery A, 246th Coast Artillery Regiment at Fort Story. In the background is one of their 16-inch Howitzers. Leading up to and throughout the war, feelings ran high against Japanese, Germans, and Italians, as well as their American-born descendants, regardless of their sentiments. (FT.)

GERMAN POWs. This group of German POWs is photographed at Weaver Fertilizer Company on April 6, 1944. During the war, 6,000 German prisoners were incarcerated at Camp Ashby in the Thalia section of Virginia Beach. Many filled jobs left vacant by American men who were shipped overseas. They worked at fertilizer plants and on area farms; only those with anti-Nazi sentiments were sent out on work details. (NPL.)

Three
MILITARY BASES
AND PRESENCE

Well before the Japanese attack on Pearl Harbor on December 7, 1941, Norfolk and Hampton Roads already felt like it was at war. The buildup had been coming for two years, and the region was flooded with military and civilian workers.

It wasn't entirely a bad thing; the ensuing war effort ended the Great Depression and raised Norfolk and the rest of the state to unprecedented levels of employment and prosperity. The many bases and posts in the region brought in more sailors and soldiers looking to spend their money.

The same bases also provided thousands of civilian jobs, and tens of millions of defense dollars poured into the area.

It was impossible to forget you were in a military town. If one didn't drive by a military installation, one stood in line at a restaurant or grocery store behind a sailor in uniform. Servicemen and their families were neighbors, co-workers, and schoolmates.

This made the war especially hard for the region. News of battles, particularly in the European Theater of Operation, brought casualty lists with familiar names. The military, according to some, had strong-armed their way into Hampton Roads but worked their way into everyone's hearts.

NAVY DAY CELEBRATION. This October 27, 1942 photo shows Norfolk celebrating the military forces at the height of the war years. Navy Day, a national celebration, was established in 1922 by the Navy League. The first year, President Warren Harding wrote, "From our earliest national beginnings the Navy has always been, and deserved to be, an object of special pride to the American people." The last Navy Day was observed in 1949. (NPL.)

ON THE BEACH. An important component of homeland security, the Coast Guard Beach Patrol, at their height, covered more than 3,700 miles of coast and employed about 24,000 men. Patrols on horseback worked in pairs, riding about 100 feet apart, usually covering a 2-mile stretch. The patrols, armed with portable radio receiver-transmitters, compasses, whistles, pistols, and rifles, were able to cover difficult terrain quickly and efficiently. The patrolmen, also called "Sand Pounders," worked the coast on foot and sometimes with the aid of leashed dogs under a program called Dogs for Defense. Especially in the early years of the war, when the threat of coastal attack by Germans was at its height, the beach patrol was an important part of American defense. (OCGS.)

GET YOUR MOTOR RUNNING. When possible, the Coast Guard Beach Patrol defended the coast with motorized vehicles. The patrol had three main wartime objectives: to detect, observe, and report offshore enemy vessels; to report enemy landing attempts; and to prevent people on shore from communicating with the enemy at sea. This patrol is seen at Kill Devil Hills on North Carolina's Outer Banks. (OCGS.)

MAINTAINING SAFE HARBORS. Port security became paramount during the war; harbors needed to remain safe and vessels protected from explosives and sabotage. Often civilian vessels were used and became part of the Coast Guard Reserve, as indicated by the "CGR" on this boat's bow. Port security duties included examining ships and sealing their radios, issuing identification cards, fighting fires, supervising loading of explosives, and guarding facilities. (OCGS.)

THREAT FROM THE SEA. The 500-ton German U-boats threatened the U.S. coast with their 14 torpedoes. The boats carried enough oil to cruise the Atlantic Coast for two weeks without refueling. Soon after America entered the war, a U-boat sank the first ship off Cape Hatteras, North Carolina, in January 1942. By July, a convoy system, like the one shown in this photo, was used to provide safe passage of ships along the coast. (OCGS.)

OLD AND NEW LIGHTHOUSES TOWERING OVER CONVALESCENT HOSPITAL, FORT STORY. Cape Henry, and Cape Charles 15 miles north, form the gateway to the Chesapeake Bay. Because of this location, Fort Story became an important first line of defense against potential enemy invasion during the war. Also, because of possible invasion, the expansion of a base hospital was seen as necessary to care for possible wounded. (AJC.)

BIG GUNS IN ACTION AT FORT STORY, CAPE HENRY, NEAR NORFOLK, VIRGINIA. Located at Cape Henry, the site where the English settlers of Jamestown first set foot on New World soil, Fort Story, a sub-installation of the U.S. Army Transportation Center and Fort Eustis, is located on some 1,451 oceanfront acres. It started out quite a bit smaller and has grown over time. In 1914, the fort (then called Cape Henry Military Reservation) began when 345 acres of land were turned over by the State of Virginia to the federal government for the establishment of an army post. In 1916, it was named for Maj. Gen. John P. Story, who once was an artillery commander at Fort Monroe. Its strategic location at the mouth of the Chesapeake Bay was perfect for staging coastal defense. During the war years, the Second Coast Artillery was headquartered here, along with National Guard units. (AJC.)

BAY WATCH. On the Cape Charles side of the Chesapeake Bay, Fort Winslow was built in 1941; the name changed to Fort John Custis in 1942. Along with Fort Story (depicted in this 1941 postcard), Fort Custis (under the command of Fort Monroe during the war years, Fort Story afterwards) protected the 15-mile wide entrance to the bay. The fort closed in 1948, and Cape Charles Air Force Station opened there in 1949, closing in 1980. (FT.)

FORT EUSTIS. This vintage drawing shows the important role Fort Eustis, located in Newport News (on land originally owned by John Rolfe, husband of Pocahontas), has in army transportation. The Transportation Corps was created in 1942, and in 1950, Fort Eustis became the U.S. Army Transportation Center and Fort Eustis. Today, Fort Eustis is the home of the U.S. Army Transportation Corps and the Transportation Corps Regiment. (PEH.)

FOUR WHEELS AND READY TO ROLL. Fort Eustis was established in Newport News in 1918 (initially as Camp Abraham Eustis, named for the first commanding officer of Fort Monroe) to serve as a point of concentration, organization, training, and embarkation for Coast Artillery Corps troops heading abroad. In World War II, the mission evolved to include army transportation training (as shown in this vintage photo of General Purpose Trucks: GPs or Jeeps), research and development, engineering, and operations, including aviation and marine shipping activities. In 1943, Fort Eustis was also used as a German prisoner-of-war camp. Today, Fort Eustis is the Transportation Corps Training Center, providing training in rail, marine, and amphibian operations and other modes of transportation; it is one of 16 Training and Doctrine Command Installations. (Library of Congress.)

OLD POINT COMFORT, VA.

OLD POINT COMFORT AND FORT MONROE. In 1609, colonists recognized the strategic location of Point Comfort and built Fort Algernourne. Other forts came and went, but with the nation reeling from the burning of Washington, D.C., by the British in the War of 1812, the importance of coastal defenses was underscored, and construction on Fort Monroe was begun in 1819. Its mission was to protect the entrance to Hampton Roads Harbor and the port cities in the region. The importance of coastal defense became apparent again in World War II, when German U-boats cruised just to the east in the Atlantic waters. This vintage postcard shows battleships passing by Fort Monroe and the Old Point Comfort lighthouse. (AJC.)

SHOOT 'EM OUT OF THE SKY. This 1942 photo shows one of the 3-inch anti-aircraft guns of Battery No. 2 at Fort Monroe. During the war, Fort Monroe was headquarters for a large array of coast artillery guns, ranging from 3-inch rapid fire guns to 16-inch guns capable of firing a 1-ton projectile 25 miles. It also controlled submarine barriers and underwater mine fields. (OCGS.)

FORT WOOL. This small man-made island, originally called Fort Calhoun, was built in 1818 to protect Hampton Roads Harbor and saw action in the Civil War. During World War II, it was under the command of Fort Monroe, and an aircraft radar station, anti-aircraft searchlights, and other features were added. A submarine net also stretched to Fort Monroe to close off the harbor entrance. Decommissioned in 1967, it is now a park (see *www.hampton.va.us/parks/fort_wool.html*) and is open for tours. (OCGS.)

Welcome Home

CAMP PATRICK HENRY, VA.
HAMPTON ROADS
PORT of EMBARKATION

CAMP PATRICK HENRY. Operating from December 1, 1942, through January 31, 1945, on 1,700 acres of land in Newport News (the site of today's Newport News/Williamsburg International Airport), this was a staging area for up to 85,000 personnel at a time, with a shuttle rail service shipside to the Hampton Roads Port of Embarkation. It was also used as a repository to welcome returning soldiers. Almost 1.5 million people passed through the camp. (Carl Warren Weidenburner.)

FULL ACCOMMODATIONS. Personnel awaiting shipment overseas or returning from Europe found Camp Patrick Henry with a large rail yard (where soldiers would board a Norfolk & Western train, as seen in this photo, to be transported between the camp and the Hampton Roads Port of Embarkation), barracks, theatre, hospital, mess hall, gymnasium, commissary, and even a nightclub. (NNWIA.)

HEADING OUT OVER THERE.
It was not just sailors and
soldiers who shipped out from
the Hampton Roads Port of
Embarkation; these tanks are
lashed to flatcars after being
processed for shipment
overseas. The docks were
commanded by Brig. Gen.
John R. Kilpatrick, who had
run Madison Square Garden
prior to the port's reactivation
on June 15, 1942. (OCGS.)

**HAMPTON ROADS PORT OF
EMBARKATION.** This historical
marker, near the Victory Arch,
reads in part: "During World War
II, 1,667,000 people passed through
here from June 15, 1942 to
September 1, 1945." During those
years, 12 million tons of cargo were
also dispatched on more than 3,000
ships. The shipments of troops and
material ranked it the third largest
port, behind only New York and
San Francisco. (PEH.)

LANGLEY AIR FORCE BASE. Established in 1917 as Langley Field (for aviation pioneer Samuel Pierpont Langley), the base grew in World War II to include a mission to develop (at laboratories, like that shown in this 1940s photo) special detector equipment used in antisubmarine warfare. These units played an important role in sinking many enemy subs off the U.S. coast during the war. (VASC.)

THE P-38 LIGHTNING. These planes were frequent sights at Langley Field during World War II; the plane was assigned to the 27th Pursuit Squadron in July 1941, the first in the U.S. Army Air Force's inventory. Langley would play a rich role in aviation during World War II, including flying the first combat sorties of the war in November 1942. The designation as Langley Air Force Base came in 1948. (Library of Congress.)

NORFOLK NAVAL SHIPYARD. Built as the Gosport Shipyard in 1767, Norfolk Naval Shipyard is located in Portsmouth, but it was renamed "Norfolk" in 1862 after the largest city in the area. The yard's employment peak of nearly 43,000 workers was reached during World War II, when the yard built nearly 30 major vessels and repaired 6,850 U.S. and Allied ships. It also built 20 tank landing ships and 50 medium landing craft. (HRNM.)

LAUNCHING OF THE SHANGRI-LA. The February 24, 1944 launching of the aircraft carrier *Shangri-La* (CV 38) drew an estimated crowd of 100,000—one of the largest ever in the history of wartime launchings at the Norfolk Naval Shipyard (NNSY). The NNSY, along with Newport News Shipbuilding, kept the economy going with such projects, becoming two of the region's largest employers; Newport News Shipbuilding went from 13,000 workers in 1939 to 70,000 in 1943. (NPL.)

SHIP BUILDING AND SHIP REPAIRS. The area shipyards, Norfolk Naval Shipyard and Newport News Shipbuilding, were involved in more than just construction; they also repaired vessels, such as the USS *Montana*, shown here in dry dock at NNSY following the June 1, 1943 collision off Cape Henry with the liberty ship USS *John Morgan*. Note the huge hole in its side and burned-out bridge area. (HRNM.)

SAINT HELENA TRAINING STATION. This vintage postcard shows the Saint Helena Reservation/Naval Training Station in Berkley, which had sat idle since 1917. During World War II, it was expanded as an auxiliary navy yard for the repair of small vessels and included barracks and a mess hall to house and feed men as their attached ships underwent work. Today, it is NNSY's Saint Helena Annex. (NPL.)

SHELTON (U. S. Route 60) NORFOLK 11, VIRGINIA

U.S. Navy Armed Guard School at Camp Shelton. Established October 1941, this school combat-trained thousands of naval officers and men who served aboard merchant ships like cargo carriers, tankers, and troop ships to defend their vessel should there be an attack by enemy sub or aircraft. Built on farmland in Norfolk near Camp Bradford, the camps today are part of Little Creek Amphibious Base. (AJC.)

1301—L. S. T. Unloads General Sherman Tanks.   *Greetings From* A. T. B., Camp Bradford, Va.

Tanks A Lot. A Landing Ship Tank (LST) unloads a General Sherman tank at Amphibious Training Base (ATB) Camp Bradford, which would later become part of Naval Amphibious Base Little Creek. Originally, Camp Bradford was designated as a training base for Seabees, but it changed its mission to training of amphibious assault tactics in 1943. (AJC.)

2030   Hitting the Beach, Amphibious Training Base, Little Creek, Virginia.

HITTING THE BEACH, AMPHIBIOUS TRAINING BASE, LITTLE CREEK, VIRGINIA. Naval Amphibious Base (NAB) Little Creek was established as a base for the vessels needed to maintain the minefields in the Chesapeake Bay Harbor Defense System; before World War II, the mine staging area was at Fort Monroe. It grew from four bases: the Amphibious Training Base, the Naval Frontier Base, and Camps Shelton and Bradford. (AJC.)

WE BUILD AND FIGHT WITH ALL OUR MIGHT!

SEABEES

UNITED STATES NAVAL CONSTRUCTION BATTALIONS

"WE BUILD AND FIGHT WITH ALL OUR MIGHT!" This topical postcard highlights the mission of the United States Naval Construction Battalions (CBs), or Seabees. Men from construction trades were recruited for the Seabees beginning in January 1942. After three weeks' training (which included light arms) at Camp Allen in Norfolk (and later at Camp Peary, Virginia), Seabees put their talents to use in the urgent need for naval construction. (AJC.)

CAMP ASHBY. Also known as Camp Thalia for the Virginia Beach neighborhood where it was located, this post began as a tent city and grew to include prefabricated buildings and other infrastructures. Soldiers here practiced combat situations, and later the post was used as a German prisoner-of-war camp. The Germans would work in area plants or on farms. After the war, many liked America so well that they applied for citizenship. (OCGS.)

AUNT SARAH. Aunt Sarah (note the sergeant's stripes on her sleeve; an honorary title) and 1st Sgt. Norman Phillips of the 111th Infantry of the Pennsylvania National Guard are pictured at Camp Ashby in 1942 or 1943 in this photograph. She came to camp almost every night with cookies and other treats for the boys; they in turn drove her shopping and wired her house for electricity. "She was adopted by the whole outfit," said Phillips. (OCGS.)

eneral Drum & Staff inspecting the 244th C.A.N.G. - Camp Pendleton, Va

CAMP PENDLETON. Established in 1912 as a rifle range to be used by state troops, this camp has been known by many names: Camp Trinkle, Camp Byrd, Camp Pollard, Camp Perry, and Camp Price. It was federalized during World War II (this vintage photo shows Lt. Gen. Hugh A. Drum, commander of the First Army Area and the Eastern Defense Command, inspecting the 244th Coast Artillery Regiment at the camp) and used as a Coast Artillery Training Center, firing practice rounds out into the Atlantic. The house in the background of this photo was the home of Anne Henry; it was taken over during the war and used as an officer's club. The federal government returned the camp to the State of Virginia in 1948. It is classified today as a State Military Reservation and primarily used by the Virginia National Guard; when you drive by, many of the World War II–era barracks and other buildings are still visible. (OCGS.)

NAVAL OPERATING BASE NORFOLK. The above September 1944 photo is an aerial view of Naval Operating Base (NOB) Norfolk, now Naval Station Norfolk. The bottom photo is a shot of the naval base piers of the same era. The land on which the station is built was the site of the 1907 Jamestown Exposition and remained abandoned until the United States entered World War I and land was purchased to develop the base. When World War II broke out, the NOB was 236 acres with two small operating areas, Chambers Field and West Landing Field, and millions of dollars were set aside for expansion. Willoughby Bay was dredged for seaplane operations, marshlands were reclaimed, the old Norfolk airport was acquired, the hospital capacity was doubled, and about 10,000 new recruits were added to the 30,000-plus already there. (HRNM.)

ANCHORS AWAY. In June 1941, the personnel at NOB Norfolk (the designation Naval Station Norfolk wouldn't come until 1953) grew by 10,000, joining the 15,559 officers and enlisted on station and the 14,426 sailors assigned to ships home-ported in Norfolk. Just prior to the start of the war, the USS *Oklahoma*, shown in the above postcard, was part of the Atlantic Fleet in Norfolk; in the late 1930s, it was transferred to the West Coast, then to Pearl Harbor, where it took three torpedo hits almost immediately after the first Japanese bombs fell; more than 400 died. The bottom photo shows two battleships at a pier at NOB in 1945. (OCGS, HRNM.)

EXERCISES AT THE OLD JAMESTOWN EXPOSITION BUILDING. Sailors practice combat maneuvers at the Naval Operating Base in front of one of the old Jamestown Exposition buildings in this 1941 photograph. The base was built on the site of the former 1907 celebration; some of the structures still stand today and are highlighted on a tour of the installation (see page 125). World War II dramatically changed the landscape of NOB. (NPL.)

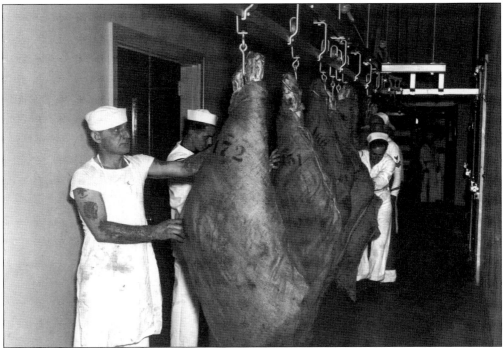

SOMEONE'S IN THE MESS HALL WITH COOKY. This navy cook knows beef is what's for dinner, as shown in this March 1940 photograph. Every job was important, but the status of cook must have been elevated a bit after a soldier or sailor had been on a steady diet of packaged food, like the army's C-rations—a stable, palatable combat ration that included a meat product and more packaged in 12-ounce rectangular cans. (NPL.)

AIR SUPERIORITY. The impact of Naval Operating Base (NOB) Norfolk in World War II is far-reaching: with only a few exceptions, all navy air squadrons that fought in the war trained in Norfolk. The air station also trained numerous British fighter squadrons and French and Russian patrol squadrons. From 1943 to the end of the war, a total of 326 U.S. units were commissioned and trained under the control of AIRLANT (Commander Air Force, Atlantic Fleet; now Naval Air Force Atlantic Fleet). The base was also involved in West Coast operations; in 1944, the year of peak production, 16 carriers, 20 carrier air groups, 57 carrier-based squadrons, 21 patrol squadrons, and 18 aviation units were deployed to the Pacific. The above 1941 photo shows Douglas Devastators at the base. The below photo shows a PBM3 in the water at the seaplane base in 1942. (HRNM.)

FLY NAVY. During World War II, Naval Operating Base (NOB) Norfolk grew exponentially. In manpower, the station leaped from an average of 2,076 officers and enlisted in December 1940 to 16,656 active duty in December 1943. For the first six months of 1943, there was an average of 700 flights per day, which represents a take-off or landing every two minutes around the clock. This made it necessary to physically grow the base, and land around it was gobbled up. Flight operations kept taking off; by 1943, the station had become the hub for a series of outlying airfields at Chincoteague, Whitehurst, Reservoir, Oceana, Pungo, Fentress, Monogram, and Creeds, Virginia, as well as Elizabeth City, Edenton, Manteo, and Harvey Point, North Carolina. The photo at right shows NOB Norfolk F6F Hellcat aviator Robert L. Brown with Scrappy. The 1943 photo below shows planes on one of the base piers awaiting loading. (HRNM.)

NEIGHBOR TO THE NORTH.
North of downtown Norfolk, out
Hampton Boulevard, lay Naval
Operating Base Norfolk. From a
few old buildings at Pine Beach,
the base grew—a large training
station was built to replace the
small school at Saint Helena
Reservation, and then a second,
even larger, station was built
beside the first. Air fields were
expanded, as well as the number
of flights (at one point, more
than 21,000 monthly). Aircraft
carriers, destroyers, battleships,
and submarines chugged past the
huge coal yards at Lamberts
Point and pulled up to one of the
dozen-plus piers at the base. It
was a portal that brought
hundreds of thousands of troops
to and through Norfolk during
the war years. The top photo
shows troops loading on a ship at
NOB in 1943; the photo at left
shows a ship berthing at NOB in
1945. (HRNM; NPL.)

A DEVASTATING ACCIDENT. On September 17, 1943, an NOB ordnance department truck was pulling four trailers loaded with depth charges on a taxiway. Each trailer was designed to carry four aerial depth charges. To save time, two additional charges were loaded on top of each trailer, which were also not properly chained down. One of the charges slipped and became wedged between the trailer and ground; the friction from being dragged caused the charge to smoke. Despite an alert marine sentry calling for assistance from a nearby fire station, the charge exploded, setting off a chain reaction of explosions from the others. Windows were shattered up to 7 miles away, and the blast was heard in Suffolk, 20 miles to the west. Some 18 buildings were damaged so badly they had to be razed, and 33 aircraft were destroyed. The damage topped $1.8 million. (HRNM.)

THE NOB EXPLOSION. The devastating accidental detonation of four trailers full of depth charges at the NOB on September 17, 1943, was felt through much of Hampton Roads and heard even further. There were almost 400 injured and 40 dead—among them S2c. Elizabeth Korensky, the only woman killed in the accident and the first WAVE (Women Accepted for Volunteer Emergency Services) to die in the line of duty in the war. Of the injured, many were left in a state of shock, with some missing large blocks of time in their memory immediately following the blast. Rebuilding was almost immediate. Six new brick barracks for troop housing were constructed, as well as R-80, the largest airplane hanger in the world. (HRNM.)

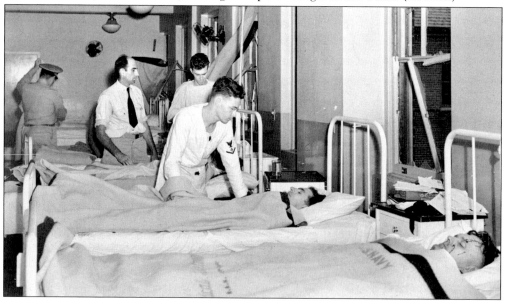

OPERATION TORCH. Operation Torch, the November 8, 1942 invasion of North Africa, was the first major amphibious action of World War II. Earlier in the year, the Nansemond Hotel in Ocean View was taken over by the federal government and became headquarters to the Amphibious Training Command, Atlantic Fleet. Troops stationed at the hotel conducted embarkation and landing exercises night and day on the shores of the Chesapeake Bay. In all, more than 40 successful assaults on enemy beaches were planned and practiced there, including Operation Torch. The hotel returned to civilian life in July 1945; it was destroyed by fire in 1980. In these photos, troops ready to head out for deployment during Operation Torch (right) and aerial landings and take-offs are practiced (below) for the assault. The assault against the occupying Germans and Vichy French was successful. (HRNM.)

LIGHTING THE WAY. The campaign to capture North Africa became paramount in 1942, as Adolf Hitler had succeeded in defeating most of Europe and, along with Italy, controlled most of the Mediterranean. His forces took the French colonial possessions in North Africa. The offensive Operation Torch, planned and practiced by the likes of Maj. Gen. George Patton in Norfolk, would be a turning point; after the loss of French Morocco, Germany remained on the defensive for the rest of the war. The operation included 5 aircraft carriers, 3 battleships, 7 cruisers, 38 destroyers, plus transport, support, and other vessels. The assault force, shown in the above photo, left Hampton Roads on October 24, 1942; the invasion took place on November 8. Almost 40,000 troops participated; 556 Americans were killed and 837 wounded, like the sailor shown in the below photo aboard the USS Solace. (HRNM.)

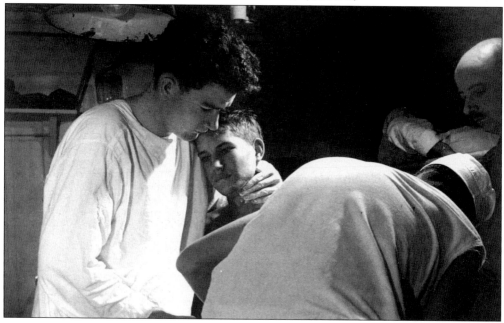

NAVAL AIR STATION OCEANA. As naval operations at Naval Operating Base Norfolk expanded, 328 acres from Potter's Farm, near the tiny community of Oceana in present-day Virginia Beach, were eyed for an auxiliary landing field (ALF) in 1940 to supplant pilot training. From the muddy field, as shown in the top picture, c. 1944, a simple triangular airfield was laid out, along with a handful of Quonset huts and a 312,000-gallon fuel storage tank. By 1942, ALF Oceana upgraded to Naval Air Auxiliary Station (NAAS). By war's end, the number of men and aircraft tripled, and in 1952, it became NAS Oceana. In the bottom photo, Bombing Squadron Three (VB-3) is shown with their Curtiss SB2C-5. Helldivers are shown at the old North Station in 1945 (the North Station closed and operations moved to the south side of the field in the mid-1950s). (NASO.)

MEETING THE DEMANDS OF WAR. As war efforts grew, so did ALF Oceana. Calls for expansion came just months after the field initially opened, and the military started eyeing adjacent farmland. Today, Oceana is more than 16 times its original size. In 1942, a new designation of Naval Air Auxiliary Station (NAAS) Oceana came. The above photo was taken at the old North Station; the photo at left of five Grumman F6F-5 Hellcats was taken over southern Virginia Beach fields. Just a few miles east of the station was Dam Neck Navy Base, which was founded in 1941 as an anti-aircraft range. Today, the facility is Fleet Combat Training Center Dam Neck and is an annex of Naval Air Station (NAS) Oceana. (NASO.)

TOUCH AND GO. Creeds Naval Outer Landing Field (NOLF) in rural Virginia Beach, as shown here, was one of many fields built in Hampton Roads to support training operations, particularly from Naval Air Station Norfolk; most would be abandoned shortly after the war. Other fields included Pungo NOLF, Whitehurst NOLF, Monogram Naval Auxiliary Air Station/Driver, Chincoteague Naval Auxiliary Air Station/Wallops Island (still open), and Auxiliary Landing Field (ALF) Fentress (still open). (PEH.)

THE NEGRO SEABEES. The military would not be desegregated until after World War II. During the war, African Americans participated in units under the premise of separate but equal, like the members of this Naval Construction Battalion, known as the Negro Seabees, in this 1942 photo. The unit trained at Camp Allen and Camp Bradford and performed similar functions as their white counterparts. (HRNM.)

PLAYING FOR KEEPS. The note with this *c.* 1942 photo reads: "Crew members who man the 20mm guns of a Coast Guard fighting ship have won an enviable reputation for gunnery results due primarily to incessant practice in assembly and operation. As expressed by the intent faces in this picture, these men play for keeps." Although the military was still segregated during the war, the conflict brought many advances for African Americans. The federal government has a policy of equal pay regardless of race for all war workers performing the same job; something that was not prevalent in the civilian world at the time. The lure of travel, good pay, and patriotism helped transform Virginia's landscape, as many African Americans left rural settings to go and see the world. When they returned, many opted to stay in Norfolk and other metropolitan areas. Total African-American representation in the military climbed as high as 701,678 in September 1944. (HRNM.)

READY FOR BATTLE. African-American mess attendants are shown in battle dress in July 1942 aboard the USS *Indianapolis*. These men had volunteered for additional duty as gunners. Commanding Officer Capt. E.W. Hanson is the second officer from the right; standing beside him is Steward William Henry. Hampton Institute, a historically black college in Hampton, Virginia, served as a training center for African-American navy enlisted personnel during World War II. (HRNM.)

NUTS AND BOLTS. African-American sailors are painting and tightening bolts on a landing craft while in training at Hampton Institute in 1945. The college served as a training center for African-American navy enlisted personnel during World War II. The boat appears to be a LCV (Landing Craft Vehicle) type. (HRNM.)

MAKING WAVES. These new Women Accepted for Volunteer Emergency Service (WAVES) are sworn in at Norfolk on October 3, 1944. WAVES was one of several auxiliary branches of the armed forces (this being navy) created for women who wanted to serve in a still all-male military. WAVES was created in 1942, and by 1943, there were 27,000 women who wore the WAVES uniform. Other branches included the U.S. Army's WACS (Women's Army Corps), the U.S. Air Force's WAAFS (Women's Auxiliary Air Force) and WASPS (Women's Air Force Service Pilots), and the Coast Guard's SPARS (*Semper Paratus*, Always Ready). (NPL.)

ROW, ROW, ROW YOUR BOAT. Women played a varied role in World War II. While some entered a military auxiliary branch, like the SPARS shown here, others took civilian jobs to assist in the war effort. Still others helped by selling war bonds, coordinating scrap drives, sewing bandages, visiting hospitals, spotting aircraft, volunteering for the Red Cross, and the like. (OCGS.)

H-45

WAC OFFICER   WAVE OFFICER   ARMY NURSE   NAVY NURSE   SPAR (COAST GUARD)   MARINE

AID TO UNIFORM IDENTIFICATION

COPYRIGHT BY
Fred Harvey

PRIDE IN UNIFORM. This vintage postcard, produced by the Fred Harvey restaurant chain during World War II, shows women's auxiliary branches in a myriad of stylish uniforms. Although the position was one of auxiliary and not full military status, many women who served as WACS, WAVES, and SPARS sometimes found themselves under fire; some were killed, and others held by the Japanese as prisoners of war. (Isle of Wight County Museum.)

ROSIE THE RIVETER. This vintage artwork, done by a Norfolk Naval Shipyard artist, depicts the important work women (personified as Rosie the Riveter) did during the war years, when many men were gone. Rosie was memorialized in a song by Redd Evans and John Jacob Loeb. The lyrics include: "All the day long whether rain or shine / She's a part of the assembly line / She's making history working for victory / Rosie the Riveter." (HRNM.)

YOU'VE COME A LONG WAY. As devastating as the war was in its own right, it also provided many opportunities, especially for women, African Americans, and other minorities, that might not have been afforded otherwise. Shown in this 1942 photo is Myrtle C. Freeman, the first woman ordnance trainee employed by the Naval Operating Base Norfolk's Naval Supply Depot. Although before World War II, there had been clear paths established for most women (homemaker, teacher, nurse), the war years changed that. With some 300,000 Virginians in uniform, women stepped into their shoes and showed they were capable of performing traditionally male jobs. For many women, the war years were their first time ever to work outside the home. Although most of those who worked in the private sector were paid less than their male counterparts, at federal installations they earned equal wages. After the war, many women workers returned to a life of domesticity, but they never gave up their sense of independence and worth. (HRNM.)

ANTISUBMARINE PATROL BRIEFING, HARVEY POINT, NORTH CAROLINA. An Auxiliary Air Station was established just south of the Virginia border near Hertford, North Carolina. Three days before Germany declared war on the United States, the German naval commander lifted all restrictions against sinking American ships; in January 1942, the U-boats sank their first boat off Cape Hatteras. (OCGS.)

INSPECTING SUBMARINE NETS. Netting designed to entrap enemy submarines was strung across the mouth of the Chesapeake Bay from Cape Henry to Cape Charles and in the inner harbor, from Willoughby Spit (near the Naval Operating Base) across to Buckroe Beach (near Fort Monroe). Guarded openings allowed friendly vessels to pass. Mine fields were also laid. No German sub penetrated the outer harbor past Cape Henry to enter the bay during the war. (AJC.)

MOTHER AND CHICKS. This photo shows the deck of a United States "tin can," navy lingo for a destroyer, on convoy duty off the Atlantic Coast on June 3, 1942, with one of the ships it is protecting in the background. The convoy system, protected by increased air coverage, was in place along the Atlantic Coast by July 1942, and no sinkings occurred the rest of the year. (HRNM.)

GERMAN GRAVES. U-boat U-85 was sunk off Cape Hatteras, North Carolina, by the U.S. destroyer *Roper* on April 14, 1942, killing all 46 aboard; 29 bodies were recovered and buried with full military honors in Hampton National Cemetery. The graves are grouped together without much information on the headstone other than the victims' names. The boat is a popular dive site today. (AJC.)

Four

ON THE HOME FRONT

There was never a single World War II battle waged on Virginia soil, but the conflict was very personal for everyone alive during the war years. The state sent some 300,000 to serve in the military; 7,000 of those would never return.

Although there was no enemy invasion, the feeling of being physically endangered was very real; all it took was to go to the oceanfront and look at the debris washed ashore from ships sunk by Nazi U-boats just a few miles out to sea. It had to be an unsettling feeling knowing the long arm of Adolph Hitler reached right to your own back door.

Local governments told citizens to be watchful and be prepared, making attack seem imminent. Citizens donned gas masks, blacked out their windows, and looked for the closest air raid shelter when in an unfamiliar part of town.

In Hampton Roads, even if a family member was not in the service, there was some military connection, for the military was all around—service members were in the long lines with you at the grocery store or movie theater, or on the crowded street car (which you had to take because rationing meant only a few gallons of gas a week.)

Many citizens turned in scrap metal and grew Victory Gardens. Women entered the work force. Everyone made do with a little less for the cause. And when the cause was won, everyone celebrated and tried to get back to a normal life on the home front.

JUST IN CASE. It was natural for folks to want to be prepared in case of enemy attack or invasion. This 1942 photo shows a gas mask demonstration by the local Defense Council, an agency that also conducted air-raid practices and coordinated blackouts. There were even orders for housewives to do "spring cleaning" in January to rid the home of as much flammable material as possible, in case incendiary bombs were dropped. (HRNM.)

SURF THE NET. For a good portion of time at the beginning of the war, the coasts of Virginia and North Carolina were on the front line as the German operation Drum Beat operated U-boats in Atlantic waters. It wasn't uncommon for residents to find debris washed ashore from one of the 66 American or Allied ships sunk by Nazi torpedoes, deck guns, or mines (a total of 79 ships were struck, and 843 merchant seamen and naval gun crewmembers lost their lives). The Germans called this time "The Great American Hunting Season." To prevent the U-boats from entering Chesapeake Bay (which would have lead them to Washington, D.C.) or Hampton Roads Harbor, submarine netting, like that shown in these photos, was used. The top image is sub netting across Willoughby Spit; the bottom image is sub netting in the York River. Nets with gateways and lines of contact mines protected the area, and channel traffic was closely monitored. (AJC.)

MARKING ANOTHER KILL. The incident of sinking another German U-boat is marked as a matter of pride and morale. Beginning in early 1942, German U-boats were a very real threat to Virginia's coast and the shipping lanes in the Atlantic. Many measures were employed to prevent attacks of maritime interests and possible land invasion, including civilians patrolling beaches and staffing watchtowers to spot the submarines. They also watched the skies for German aircraft. One method that affected most everyone was mandatory blackouts. Not only were municipal interests blocked out in this matter, but blackouts also made Allied ships more difficult for the U-boats to find without any shore lights on the horizon to silhouette them. The defense of Hampton Roads also relied on reconnaissance by yachtsmen, harbor pilots, fishermen, and civilian pilots who flew their own planes. Reports were sent back to the military via radio or, in some cases, carrier pigeon. From Langley Field, Naval Operating Base Norfolk, and other bases, observation planes and bombers also flew patrol missions to be on the lookout. (OCGS.)

USS NAECO. This American oil tanker was torpedoed, split in two, and sunk by the submarine U-124 on March 23, 1942, off Cape Lookout, North Carolina, killing 24. Vessels with drafts less than 10 feet used the Intracoastal Waterway for protection, but larger ships had to travel in open ocean, called "Torpedo Alley." Until the convoy system was put in place, Nazi submarines declared an open season on American shipping interests. (OCGS.)

USS ROBERT C. TUTTLE. Smoke billows from this ship's starboard side as it burns off Cape Henry, the result of a collision on the night of April 9, 1942, with the Norwegian freighter *Benwood*. Crews on either ship did not see each other until it was too late, since both ships were traveling with navigation lights blacked out because of U-boat activity in the area. (HRNM.)

Town Ordinance Regarding Blackout

In compliance with the Town Ordinance that the entire ocean front be blacked out at night, black curtains have been put up in each room for this purpose. These must be drawn each night before lights are turned on and kept closed until lights are out. The occupants of each room are entirely responsible, and anyone failing to comply with this ordinance will be liable to a fine.

THE POLICE DEPARTMENT.
C. E. HOBECK, Chief of Police.

LIGHTS OUT. After the Japanese attack on Pearl Harbor on December 7, 1941, the U.S. Coast Guard Auxiliary reserve flotilla was activated, beginning a round-the-clock harbor patrol. On December 9, the army put up anti-aircraft batteries and warned of possible air raids. Blackouts (indicated on this vintage postcard) went into effect four days later on December 13. In towers built along the coastal waters, volunteers stood watch, reporting every aircraft to the military. (AJC.)

PUT THE PARTY ON HOLD. This vintage postcard shows the Surf Club in Virginia Beach. In 1942, the oceanfront became an interesting, if not at times frightening, place to be, as German U-boats mined the entrance to the Chesapeake Bay and declared war on all vessels, military or commercial. Several ships and tankers exploded with massive displays of fire and smoke, all within four miles of the shoreline and in sight of the boardwalk. (OCGS.)

OIL WASHED ASHORE. This July 1942 photo taken in Virginia Beach near the Cavalier Beach Club shows oil washed ashore from a ship sunk off the coast by a German submarine. Blackouts were necessary to prevent silhouettes that aided the U-boats in finding their targets. During this time, most home and business windows were covered at night with black curtains made of oilcloth, and exterior lights were extinguished. (OCGS.)

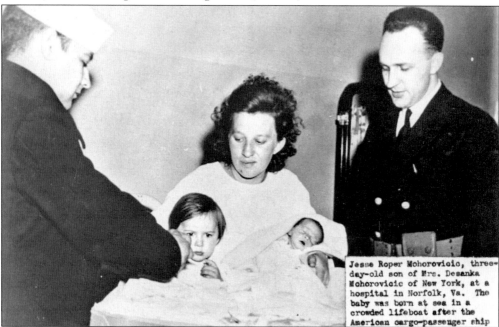

Jesse Roper Mohorovicic, three-day-old son of Mrs. Desanka Mohorovicic of New York, at a hospital in Norfolk, Va. The baby was born at sea in a crowded lifeboat after the American cargo-passenger ship

YOUNG VICTIM. The note on this 1942 photo reads in part, "Jesse Roper Mohorovicic, three-day-old son of Mrs. Desanka Mohorovicic . . . at a hospital in Norfolk, Virginia . . . was born at sea in a . . . lifeboat after the American cargo-passenger ship M/V CITY OF NEW YORK had been torpedoed . . . Jesse Roper [was] named for the destroyer USS ROPER which picked them up at sea." The March 29 attack by U-160 killed 26. (HRNM.)

SINKING OF THE SAN JACINTO. Survivors of the passenger ship *San Jacinto* arrive in Norfolk April 24, 1942, after the ship was torpedoed by U-201 two days earlier off Cape Hatteras, North Carolina. The explosion tore through staterooms; remarkably, 183 passengers and crew escaped in lifeboats and rafts, while 14 died. They waited until dawn to send a distress signal for fear they'd be attacked by another U-boat. The survivors were picked up by the USS *Rowan*. (OCGS.)

SURVIVORS OF A SHIP SINKING ON MAIN STREET. The crew in this March 1942 photo escaped with their lives when their ship was torpedoed off the coast by a U-boat. American ships had been a target of the Nazi submarines since May 21, 1941, when the freighter USS *Robin Moor* was sunk. The tragedy killed two crew members from Hampton Roads: Frank Ward Jr. from Portsmouth and Virgil Sanderlin of Norfolk. (NPL.)

SIGN OF THE TIMES. For a while, the threat of an attack by air seemed very real, and the local defense council tried to make everyday life for citizens safe by telling them what to do if the bombs started falling. If that happened when shopping at Smith & Welton's, one of the area's premier department stores, all you had to do was read the sign and, of course, "Keep Calm!" (OCGS.)

DUCK AND COVER. This air raid shelter was erected on the Norfolk City Hall lawn (now the MacArthur Memorial) during a civilian defense rehearsal in October 1941. By Gov. Colgate W. Darden Jr.'s orders, Norfolk and other vital areas of the state were required to have both a blackout and a daylight air-raid drill every month. The first area-wide daylight air-raid drill occurred on May 25, 1942. (OCGS.)

ANY PORT IN THE STORM. Civil defense workers greet people in the doorway of the Withers Building in downtown Norfolk following an air-raid drill. The daylight drills could be quite dramatic: sirens blaring across the region, streets clearing of moving cars and pedestrians, and people ducking into shelters, or makeshift shelters, as shown. Many businesses called Chief Air Raid Warden Richard M. Marshall asking for exemptions; few got them. (OCGS.)

SORTING OUT THE GOOD STUFF. Civilian defense personnel are seen here in this October 28, 1943 photo sorting through paper from a scrap drive. Many folks in Hampton Roads and across the country volunteered to defend the nation from the enemy. They trained in first aid and aircraft spotting and helped coordinate the gathering of materials useful for the war effort. By mid-1942, more than 10 million Americans were civil defense volunteers. (OCGS.)

LOOK, UP IN THE SKY. All eyes were on the skies during the war, and ears remained open, listening for air-raid sirens. These photos are from the first Hampton Roads region-wide daytime air-raid drill on May 25, 1942. The top photo shows people scrambling to get off Granby Street; the bottom photo shows a crowd gathering at Monticello Arcade awaiting the all-clear signal. The region also practiced blackouts at nights and lived through a perpetual dim-out—where many neon lights, advertising signs, and other bright bulbs were extinguished during the war years. (NPL.)

WHAT CAN I DO? After America joined the war, many folks asked that question, and many found the answer in volunteerism. Some took on paramilitary functions like air raid wardens or airplane spotters; other joined the Red Cross or coordinated scrap drives. For a while during the early part of the war, an invasion from the enemy seemed imminent. However, later it was clear the real danger would come from the sea and not the air; Germany simply didn't have long-range bombers that could reach the American coast, nor did they have any aircraft carriers, and the Japanese did not operate in the Atlantic. Still, for a while, the threat seemed real enough that air-raid drills became commonplace at work and, in this vintage photo, at school. Children were also part of the war effort, not only practicing in air-raid drills, but assisting with scrap drives, helping in Victory Gardens, and making artwork to send to soldiers and sailors overseas. (HRNM.)

AIR RAID WARDENS, REPORTING FOR DUTY. This 1942 photo shows a Norfolk Air Raid Warden section in a drill. Wardens were in neighborhoods, in the workplace, and even at department stores, should the bombs have fallen during a shopping trip. Only one bomb ever fell on Norfolk—a 235-pound big boy that had accidentally fallen from a navy plane on October 12, 1944, into the backyard of James M. Wolcott; it did not detonate. (NPL.)

GOT A LIGHT? Despite efforts to keep Hampton Roads dim during nighttime hours, the military often lit up the sky with brilliant searchlights beaming out into the night looking for enemy aircraft, like the floodlight illuminating this nighttime recruitment scene at Lee Park. There were searchlights and floodlights established across the region, including the Oceanfront, Ocean View, Dam Neck, and Camp Pendleton. (NPL.)

SPOTTERS AND PLOTTERS. Elizabeth Whitehead, left, and Elizabeth Johnson work at the information center at Aircraft Warning Service in the above photo, taken May 28, 1942; others monitor aircraft from a spotter's tower, as shown in the photo to the right. It was all done to defend the city against a possible sneak air raid. When aircraft were spotted, information such as the time, type of plane, direction of travel, and the like was relayed to workers who plotted the information on a large, war room–type map. In turn, reports were given to the military. Norfolk was the center for the state's Aircraft Warning Service, and upwards of 750 were recruited to staff the area's 15 posts. The area's service was activated June 15, 1941. (NPL; OCGS.)

KIDS OF ALL KIND DO THEIR PART.
Pipes and cans and old mattress springs
are perfect for Mr. Billy Whiskers, the
goat, and gathering for the war effort, as
shown in this September 23, 1942
photo. Local efforts to reclaim
everything from rubber to paper to
metal were overseen by Norfolk's
Committee for Conservation and
Salvage. Boy Scouts collected waste
paper, firehouses were repositories for
metal, and rubber was taken to gas
stations. (OCGS.)

SCRAP. This poster, done by artist Roy
Schatt, emphasizes the need to salvage
what was possible to reuse for the war.
Folks in Hampton Roads took the need
seriously. Two examples include the
Norfolk Boys Club fishing more than a
ton of rubber from the Lafayette River
and the Norfolk Lions Club petitioning
businesses to turn in salvage items and
collecting more than 60 tons of iron.
(Library of Congress.)

MRS. ELEPHANT HELPS OUT. An elephant from a visiting circus helps collect old cars for the scrap drive in this October 13, 1942 photo. In Hampton Roads, the United Scrap Drive was the biggest campaign of all. Boy Scouts took apart old cars for 140 tons of metal, and the town's last surviving Confederate veteran, T.N. Mayo, turned in his muzzle-loading shotgun. An average of 108 pounds per capita was collected. (NPL.)

"USE IT UP, WEAR IT OUT, MADE DO, OR DO WITHOUT." Everyone was expected to make sacrifices in World War II. Resources became rare as many items were diverted for war use, including rubber. In December 1941, a freeze was put on the sale of tires. Norfolk's city tire administrator only made exceptions for doctors, nurses, and veterinarians, if the old ones were completely threadbare. Not surprisingly, the theft of tires increased dramatically. (OCGS.)

LEE SCHOOL SCRAP DRIVE, MAY 10, 1944. Students at this Norfolk school did their patriotic duty in salvaging scrap. In addition to rounding up old paper, metal, rubber, and the like, Americans did without new things, too. Automobiles were no longer being made, and to save fabric, clothes had shorter hems and were missing cuffs on shirt sleeves and trouser legs. "Scrap" and "rations" became part of everyday vocabulary. (NPL.)

WAITING FOR GAS RATION CARDS. The line was long on May 12, 1942, as Norfolkians waited in line at Robert E. Lee School for gas ration cards. Area petrol delivery dropped one-third in 1942 from the year before, and stations opened for limited hours—and then closed altogether when the fuel ran out until next month's allotment. Folks, with few exceptions, were limited to purchasing six gallons a week. (NPL.)

OFFICE OF PRICE ADMINISTRATION

OPA Form No. R-303

No. 77816 –154

War Ration Book One

UNITED STATES OF AMERICA

WARNING

1 Punishments ranging as high as *Ten Years' Imprisonment or $10,000 Fine, or Both,* may be imposed under United States Statutes for violations thereof arising out of infractions of Rationing Orders and Regulations.

2 This book must not be transferred. It must be held and used only by or on behalf of the person to whom it has been issued, and anyone presenting it thereby represents to the Office of Price Administration, an agency of the United States Government, that it is being so held and so used. For any misuse of this book it may be taken from the holder by the Office of Price Administration.

3 In the event either of the departure from the United States of the person to whom this book is issued, or of his or her death, the book must be surrendered in accordance with the Regulations.

4 Any person finding a lost book must deliver it promptly to the nearest Ration Board.

Certificate of Book Holder

I, the undersigned, do hereby certify that I have observed all the conditions and regulations governing the issuance of this War Ration Book; that the "Description of Book Holder" contained herein is correct; that an application for issuance of this book has been duly made by me or on my behalf; and that the statements contained in said application are true to the best of my knowledge and belief.

[Book Holder's Own Name]

(Signature of, or on behalf of, Book Holder)

Any person signing on behalf of Book Holder must sign his or her own name below

and indicate relationship to Book Holder

(Father, Mother, or Guardian)

The Stamps contained in this Book are valid only after the lawful holder of this Book has signed the certificate below, and are void if detached contrary to the Regulations. (A father, mother, or guardian may sign the name of a person under 18.) In case of questions, difficulties, or complaints, consult your local Ration Board.

FOLD BACK   FOLD BACK

Certificate of Registrar

1942

This is to Certify that pursuant to the Rationing Orders and Regulations administered by the OFFICE OF PRICE ADMINISTRATION, an agency of the United States Government,

Name, Address, and Description of person to whom the book is issued:

Hitchens (Last name)   Adolphus (First name)   Eugene (Middle name)

120 (Street No. or P.O. Box No.)   Rodgers Avenue (Street or R.F.D.)

(City or town)   Norfolk (County)   Virginia (State)

5 ft. 10 in. 195 lbs. Brown (Color of eyes) Brown (Color of hair) 37 yrs. Sex Male ☒ Female ☐

has been issued the attached War Ration Stamps this 5th day of May 1942, upon the basis of an application signed by himself ☒, herself ☐, or on his or her behalf by his or her husband ☐, wife ☐, father ☐, mother ☐, exception ☐ (Check one.)

Alice Daisy Keister (Signature) (Registrar)

Local Board No. 65-1   County Norfolk   State Virginia

Stamps must not be detached except in the presence of the retailer, his employee, or person authorized by him to make delivery.

| WAR RATION STAMP 24 | WAR RATION STAMP 22 | WAR RATION STAMP 20 |
| WAR RATION STAMP 23 | | WAR RATION STAMP 19 |

WAR RATION BOOK ONE. This ration book was issued to Norfolk resident Adolphus Eugene Hitchens in 1942. Many items became scarce during the war; Americans were asked to sacrifice by having some of the everyday items we take for granted rationed out, including rubber/tires, shoes/leather, nylon and other materials, sugar, butter, shortening/lard, liquor, gasoline, vegetables, and meat. There were also limits on alcohol, cigarettes/tobacco, and even travel. Many things were hard to come by in Hampton Roads; bananas virtually disappeared. Those that remained (only 14 in all of Norfolk by one official count) cost 75¢ each instead of the usual dime. Coffee deliveries were cut by 25%. Restaurants limited the amount of sugar one could put in coffee to one spoonful per cup. There was even a shortage on Coca-Cola. The government set up the Office of Price Administration (OPA) to regulate the rationed products and issued these books of stamps to "purchase" the products in short supply. When the stamps were gone, you did without until the next month, unless you purchased them on the black market. (AJC.)

OUT OF GAS. Service stations in Norfolk and across the country were under rationing, too. When the station ran out, it closed until more came in. Although many shortages were more a gastronomic nuisance, restrictions on the use of cars was a real quality-of-life issue, forcing many onto the already crowded city buses and streetcars, if they could find a place to sit or stand. One official asked folks to walk to work. (OCGS.)

C.J. JOHNSON FRETS OVER THE MEAT SHORTAGE. This Norfolk butcher worries about meat supply in this vintage photo. The Office of Price Administration (OPA) reduced slaughterhouse production in the last quarter of 1942 by 30%, and soon shelves in Hampton Roads and across the country went bare. A spokesman for the food industry said Norfolk had only 30 percent of the beef and pork it needed. Even so, what was already scarce was also rationed. (NPL.)

RUNNING LOW. Slaughtering quotas made the meat supply run low, and what was available cost plenty in rationing stamps. Hampton Roads was spared a meat famine because of a thriving black market, which was supplied by Tidewater farmers who increased the number of hogs and cattle they slaughtered to sell at premium prices. This Norfolk butcher looks like he would like to have some of the black market beef. (OCGS.)

MAKING SENSE OF IT ALL. Understanding how the points worked on rationing stamps took skill and patience. Newport News women in this vintage photo learn how to effectively ration through a workshop. Also, the Norfolk Nutrition Committee started holding "Foods for Victory" classes in 1943, teaching how to make a complete set of well-balanced menus for the month, as well as how to can food from the Victory Garden. (Library of Congress.)

HOW DOES YOUR GARDEN GROW? Little Brucie Tyler, seven, stands in her grandmother's Victory Garden in the Lochhaven neighborhood of Norfolk in 1943. The city's Victory Garden Committee estimated that 30,000 gardens were planted in Norfolk in 1943 and that home gardens increased the vegetable supply in the area by 50%. Schools were encouraged to grow food for their own lunchroom, and the city provided the soil and fertilizer for the effort. (FT.)

BAYVIEW SCHOOLCHILDREN WORKING ON A VICTORY GARDEN. Students are shown tending their garden in this April 2, 1943 photo. Victory Gardens were planted in empty lots, on rooftops, and in backyards to help stave off the wartime food shortage. Some produce was eaten right away; some was canned for later use. Many recipe books came out highlighting fruits and vegetables grown most often in Victory Gardens. (NPL.)

CAN IT. *Time* magazine reported in its February 8, 1943 issue: "The Agriculture Department hopes that, because of Victory gardens (as many as 18 million of them), food rationing will have much less sting this summer. The department emphasizes that gardening is work as well as fun, requires sound planning as well as patriotism." To help local families, the Norfolk Civilian Defense's Nutrition Committee held "Foods for Victory" cooking classes and taught how to can. The agency even purchased 40 high-quality pressure cookers, which they rented out to persons who needed them. The man in the photo below is recycling cooking grease and lard. (NPL.)

I SELL WAR BONDS. That's what this woman's hat says, as she solicits business from servicemen in downtown Norfolk in this 1943 photograph. The cost of war was expensive and could not be financed by income tax alone. Folks in Hampton Roads and across the nation were encouraged to buy war bonds at every payday and, as the poster in this photo prompts, to "Ask about our payroll savings plan." The region responded to the call to not only volunteer their time, but invest their hard-earned dollars in the war effort. There were countless war bond drives in the area, at one point raising $37.5 million to pay for a cruiser to be named the USS *Norfolk*. One remarkable story tells of a Russian immigrant, Sam Sutton, who owned a confectionery store on Park Avenue in Norfolk. He felt so strongly about war bonds, he gave a passionate speech at a civic club and sold $7,000 in bonds that night. He went on to push the effort, selling more than $1 million in war bonds by the time he was through. (OCGS.)

ELIAS CODD. Like Sam Sutton, Elias Codd was another immigrant from Europe who felt strongly about America and the sale of bonds to fund the war movement. Codd is shown in these photos at his delicatessen on Princess Anne Road. The above photo was taken in 1942; the bottom photo is from 1943. He would take orders from customers and go and stand patiently in line for them to purchase their bonds. He eventually sold more than $3 million in war bonds and was recognized as one of the country's outstanding bond salesmen. (NPL.)

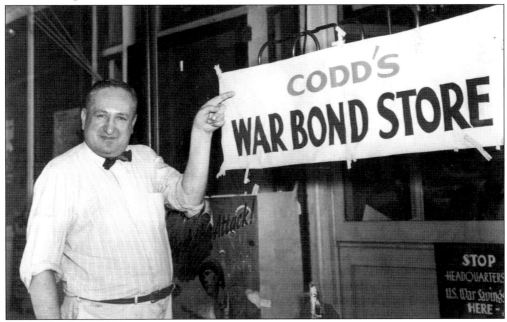

BOND RALLY ON GRANBY STREET. This July 17, 1942 photo shows a rally on Norfolk's Granby Street to excite folks into buying war bonds. In Hampton Roads and across the nation, movie stars and other personalities were used to promote the sale of war bonds, with Kate Smith and Carole Lombard being two of the most famous. (NPL.)

"NORFOLK WELCOMES EVERYBODY IN UNIFORM." So says this vintage billboard from the Norfolk Citizens Committee. Although there were tensions between the military and civilian population at time, folks in Hampton Roads accepted and then embraced the important role it was playing in World War II. Citizens not only supported the military through war-bond purchases, but also through volunteerism in a number of capacities, like the United Service Organization (USO) and the Red Cross. (PEH.)

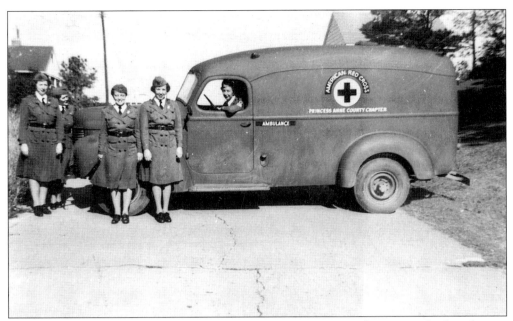

AMERICAN RED CROSS—PRINCESS ANNE COUNTY CHAPTER. Folks got involved in the war effort in many ways, including, in this early 1940s photo, pictured from left to right, Mrs. Pinky Willis, Mrs. Rumbee, Mrs. Museevy, Mrs. Vaughn, Mrs. Floyd, and Mrs. Darmiere at wheel. Princess Anne County is the current city of Virginia Beach. The women would have worked on civil defense, helped with nursing, and visited the boys in the hospital. (OCGS.)

THE SMITH STREET USO. One of the area's USO offices was on Smith Street in Norfolk; the center opened March 15, 1942. The recreation center finally addressed the needs of African-American sailors and soldiers in the area; all other USOs had been segregated. In this 1944 photo, USO volunteers are shown entertaining officers from the carrier *Shangri-La*, which was constructed at the nearby Norfolk Naval Shipyard. (NPL.)

WRAP IT UP. Volunteers at the Navy YMCA wrap packages for service members in this vintage photograph. The Navy YMCA was located on Brooke Avenue in Norfolk and offered leisure with a religious twist, in contrast to the beer halls and burlesque shows around the corner on Granby Street. There was also a Navy Y Beach Club at Ocean View for the aquatic crowd. (OCGS.)

MAY I HAVE THIS DANCE? This early 1940s photo shows a dance in Norfolk's old Municipal Building sponsored by the local USO. There were eight area USOs to offer recreation for sailors and soldiers, including the Salvation Army USO at Plume and Granby Streets and the Smith Street USO, which was available for African-American service members. Social events like dancing helped keep the mind off the war, at least for one evening. (NPL.)

CUTTING A RUG. A jitterbug team dances in a friendly competition at the Smith Street USO in this 1942 photo. There were eight USOs in Hampton Roads during World War II, but others were segregated; the Smith Street USO offered recreation for African Americans. Newport News native and jazz great Pearl Bailey toured with the USO from 1941 to her death in 1990, no doubt belting out danceable ditties. (NPL.)

SALVATION ARMY USO. These early 1940s photographs show sailors and soldiers relaxing and enjoying themselves at the Salvation Army USO. The above photo shows the center's snack bar; the below photo was taken at a party. This USO was something to write home about: in February 1942, it reopened after $75,000 in renovations. The elaborate center provided 125 beds, including 20 set aside for visiting parents or relatives. On the first floor was a large canteen seating 80, and a recreation room was on the seventh floor. The center held dances and provided 350 pairs of roller skates for some fast-paced entertainment. There were events offered every night of the week. The Salvation Army USO, staffed with local volunteers, epitomized the warmth and hospitality Hampton Roads felt for their military citizens. (NPL.)

HAVE A DOUGHNUT, BOYS. Salvation Army USO volunteer Peggy Koons feeds the boys in blue in this 1943 photo. Started in 1942 by the Pilot Club and the Sons and Daughters of Liberty, a "bottomless" cookie barrel provided homemade treats for visiting sailors and soldiers. Later, Koons and her friends formed the Norfolk Women's Council of the Navy League to act as hostesses for enlisted men and officers. The USO was formed at the request of President Franklin D. Roosevelt in 1941, who said it would be best if private organizations handled the on-leave recreation for the armed forces. Six agencies formed the USO: the Salvation Army, YMCA, YWCA, National Catholic Community Services, National Travelers Aid Association, and the National Jewish Welfare Board. During World War II, there were more than 3,000 USOs worldwide, offering service members a place to dance, meet people, see movies, talk, write letters, and have a cup of coffee and a doughnut. (NPL.)

TOUCHDOWN! There was always something going on for the military in Hampton Roads. In this November 14, 1942 photo, area sailors are treated to a football game between the College of William and Mary (W&M) and Virginia Military Institute (VMI) at Foreman Field at W&M's Norfolk Campus (now Old Dominion University). At any given time, there were between 10,000 and 15,000 sailors and soldiers on leave or off duty. (NPL.)

ENJOYING THE SIGHTS HERE...

ENJOYING THE SIGHTS HERE. R&R (rest and relaxation) often meant a trip to the beaches at the Virginia Beach Oceanfront, Ocean View in Norfolk, or Buckroe Beach in Hampton. This vintage postcard shows a sailor on leave enjoying the natural beauty of Hampton Roads. In addition to local United Service Organizations, area municipalities also offered recreation departments to offer visiting sailors some fun. (OCGS.)

STARS AND STRIPES FOREVER. U.S. Coast Guard Chief Specialist J. Philip Sousa II, son of the famous band leader, strikes up his band in this March 19, 1943 visit to Norfolk. There were many forms of entertainment available for the armed forces, such as band performances and dances. The region saw the likes of Glenn Miller, Benny Goodman, Harry James, and Count Basie. (OCGS.)

MORBID CURIOSITY. Following the end of the war, the automobile of Commander-in-Chief of the Luftwaffe, President of the Reichstag, Prime Minister of Prussia, and Adolf Hitler's designated successor, Hermann Goering, was put on display at Norfolk's Selden Arcade on December 11, 1945. Such displays were often used as a way to raise money for the war effort, or to help settle the war debt, by charging admission either in cash or by selling war stamps or bonds. (NPL.)

WAR TROPHY. This captured Japanese submarine made its way to Norfolk's Freemason Street on March 26, 1943, to be showcased as a trophy of war. The event was also used as a fund-raiser for war stamps and bonds. Notice curiosity seekers lining up for a peek in the sub and volunteers in the bottom of the photo taking cash for war-bond purchases, a cash register strategically placed. Many techniques were used to increase war bond sales, including parading war icons such as this, rallies with entertainment, and the appearance of movie stars and other famous folks. (NPL; OCGS.)

PRINCESS ANNE GOLF CLUB, AND COTTAGES, VIRGINIA BEACH, VA.   4754

CONFISCATED BUILDINGS. Several area buildings were needed for the war effort and were temporarily occupied by the military during World War II. Among them is the Cavalier, shown in this 1941 postcard. The upscale hotel was used as a radar training school. The Cavalier Hotel, built in 1927, quickly became the premiere hotel in Virginia Beach. Known as "the Aristocrat of Virginia's Shore," it has attracted presidents and stars of the stage and screen. It was the nation's leading hostelry from the 1930s through the 1950s, with Bette Davis, Ginger Rogers, Bing Crosby, and Betty Grable among the hotel's distinguished guests. The Cavalier's exclusive Beach Club was the world's largest hirer of big bands during this time as well, with performers such as Benny Goodman and Cab Calloway. It was the location and facilities that drew the navy to the Cavalier until 1945. Another grand hotel, the Nansemond, in Norfolk's Ocean View, was used during the planning of Operation Torch. It also was occupied until 1945. The Cavalier still stands today; the Nansemond burned in 1980. (OCGS.)

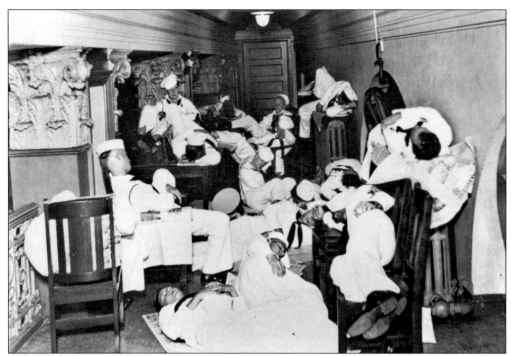

NO REST FOR THE WEARY. As Norfolk's military population boomed, sailors were often seen taking catnaps almost anywhere in public, like these navy boys catching 20 at the Norfolk YMCA. World War II brought a severe housing shortage as sailors and civilian defense workers streamed into Norfolk. Tenants doubled up in homes and learned to "hot bed," or sleep in shifts. (HRNM.)

NAVY HOUSING. Benmoreell, (named after Rear Adm. Ben Moreell), shown in this vintage photograph, was a navy housing project for enlisted men. The site was crowded—603 structures on 77 acres—and built quickly and inexpensively for temporary lodging; however, more than a million families called it home from 1941 to 1993. It has been torn down and rebuilt. Ample, adequate housing was always a problem during the war. (NPL.)

ALEXANDER PARK. This fall 1942 photo shows Alexander Park, near Norfolk Naval Shipyard in Portsmouth, a civilian worker housing project still under construction; the demountable houses have almost been completed. NNSY payroll jumped from 7,625 to 42,893 during the war, and the area was hard-pressed to accommodate the new workers and their families, although Alexander Park and 45 other war-housing projects tried to help fill the void. (HRNM.)

BROAD CREEK VILLAGE. Shown in this December 2, 1943 photo, Broad Creek in Norfolk was a 507-acre housing project for the wartime surplus of military families. It was one of the nation's largest defense housing projects and Norfolk's first pre-fabricated housing, scheduled to be demounted and moved within six months of the war's end; it was in use until 1958. The community was self-sustaining, with schools, fire and police, shopping, and parks. (NPL.)

HEWITT FARMS. This was another housing project, located in Norfolk's Ocean View, designed to accommodate the huge numbers moving into the region during World War II. Nearly 15,000 homes were finished in Norfolk alone during the last four months of 1942, but it still was not enough. To oversee the best use of all the new homes, the National Housing Agency established a War Housing Center in Norfolk. (HRNM.)

WARTIME HOUSING IN NORFOLK, MAY 12, 1943. Housing in the community was hopelessly inadequate, and dozens of public and private housing projects were continually ongoing in Hampton Roads during the war years. In 1941, Norfolk's population doubled with the hundreds of military families moving into the area, as more than 100,000 came and decided to stay a while. (OCGS.)

AT HOME IN LEWIS PARK. The housing situation reached near-emergency proportions in Hampton Roads during World War II. To help, some 200 trailers were brought in at Lewis Park, across Hampton Boulevard from Benmoreell, shown here December 3, 1942. Twenty-five of the trailers were expandable, where seven could sleep or two could live; the rest had room for only four persons. (OCGS.)

DON'T LOSE YOUR MARBLES. Everyone in Hampton Roads felt overcrowded. Because of the influx of military and their families during the war, housing was inadequate, and there were long lines wherever you went. The only solace might have been a friendly game of marbles, like the boys in this *c.* 1943 photo are playing in front of temporary-housing trailers in Norfolk's Ocean View. Note the amusement park's roller coaster in the background. (NPL.)

"WE CAN DO IT!" That's the message Rosie the Riveter has to women in this war-era poster by artist J. Howard Miller. On the home front, women took on a myriad of roles, many in addition to their traditional responsibilities. Locally, some of the non-military tasks fell under the direction of the Hampton Roads Area Office of the War Manpower Commission (WMC), who said there were 30,000-plus women in the region and wanted to hire at least half of them into war jobs. The navy yard hired up to 1,000 women in its shops, and the naval air station trained female mechanics to repair planes. Women drove Virginia Electric Power Company (VEPCO) streetcars and concrete-mixer trucks. The June 1942 photo below shows two women truck drivers that look more than willing and able to tackle the task ahead of them. (Library of Congress; NPL.)

I Do. The happy couple in this war-era photo celebrates just tying the knot at the Salvation Army USO in Norfolk. Many young couples (some still teenagers) felt the urgency to marry before the sailor or soldier was shipped out on deployment. Weddings were often hastily arranged and unceremoniously performed. Hundreds of thousands married; a record number of marriages occurred in the first two years of the war. (OCGS.)

WAR BRIDES. This vintage photo shows a group of war brides debarked from the USS *Benjamin Williams* at Norfolk Army Base and passing through the Hampton Roads Port of Embarkation, bound for Tunis. During World War II, there was an average of a 20% increase in marriage, a contributing factor to increased birth rates and the Baby Boomer generation. (NPL.)

I LOVE THE NIGHTLIFE. There were some elements that tugged on sailors to let go and have some fun while in port. Beer halls and burlesque shows were the mildest forms of vice along Granby Street, pictured in the 1940s postcard at left and on East Main Street in Norfolk. Other vices included prostitution, gambling, and brawls. The story of Elvira Taylor, one of the nation's most famous "Allotment Annies," combines a little of all that. Taylor married six sailors and was on the seventh when arrested after two of her "husbands" fought at a bar after showing each other the picture of their "wife." Taylor was in it for their navy pay and potential life insurance. Another vice was tattoos, as shown in the below vintage photo of a body art parlor along Granby Street; after all, what's a sailor without "Mom" emblazoned across his forearm? (OCGS; Library of Congress.)

VIRGINIA BEACH, VA.   DEC. 1940

SIGNS OF THE TIMES. There was on-again, off-again tension between the military and civilian population in Hampton Roads, as it was with many towns with a military presence. The 1940s sign above, "No Dogs or Sailors Allowed on Grass," posted in Virginia Beach, is an indication of barely tolerating the navy in town. Although the military did bring jobs, money, and security, it also used many resources, not all of which were plentiful. That, coupled with the occasional sailor or soldier out on the town while on leave and giving into the temptation of wine, women, or song, upset many locals (especially those with teenage daughters). Rest assured, many sailors were just sowing a few wild oats, and most indiscretions were minor. They were also under the watchful eye of the Shore Patrol, as shown in the bottom war-era photo. (NPL.)

PLAYING SOLDIER. Young Fielding Tyler, 10, now retired army and director of the Old Coast Guard Station Museum, is seen in this 1943 photo with his seven-year-old sister, Brucie, at their Lochhaven home in Norfolk. Kids, many of whom had fathers off to war, got into the patriotic act, emulating what they saw in the newspaper or heard on the radio. (FT.)

"JUST A LITTLE SOMETHING TO REMEMBER PEARL HARBOR." This postcard, marked June 1943 at Oceana, Virginia, was indicative of many Americans' sentiments during the war towards Japan, Germany, and Italy. Often these feelings were expressed with language or images that would be found offensive today, but it is hard to judge the words and actions of a nation at war some 60 years ago by current standards. (HRNM.)

PINT-SIZED PATRIOTISM. The children in this Norfolk neighborhood, c. 1943, above, show their patriotic colors by making kites in support of America and the war effort. Front-and-center is an Uncle Sam flag. Children helped in the war effort in many ways, assisting in the Victory Gardens, with scrap/salvage drives, and keeping spirits up on the home front. In the bottom photo, kids flock around this searchlight at Lee Park in Norfolk on October 3, 1941. Children were naturally curious, and sometimes anxious, about what was happening in the war abroad and at home. (NPL.)

A Soldier Comes Home. A Norfolk family has gone all out to welcome home their returning hero, Joe, as shown in this May 18, 1945 photo. All across Hampton Roads, similar scenes were played out as shiploads of sailors and soldiers started returning home by the end of June 1945. For a while, amid all the V-E Day and V-J Day celebrations and all the homecoming parties, the problems Hampton Roads had faced over the past almost five years—housing shortages, food shortages, rationing, blackouts, air-raid drills, and overcrowding everywhere—faded. There was dancing in the streets, and excited girls kissed navy men to show their appreciation for peace. When all was said and done, the nation was forever changed, and Hampton Roads was no different. In fact, it was filling its role as a military town even in victory; after the dust settled, Norfolk still was the world's largest naval base, a title worn proudly even today. (NPL.)

Five

V-E Day, V-J Day, and the War's Aftermath

The war had been raging for more than three years when the spring of 1945 rolled around. Hampton Roads was war-weary. Norfolk looked as tired as the people felt: the overuse of the infrastructure was taking its toll, and buildings, roads, and the like were dirty, broken, and in shambles.

It was President Harry S Truman who brought the news of victory in Europe on May 8, the day after Germany surrendered. Bells, whistles, sirens, and horns blared across the area in celebration. Within a month, ships streamed into Hampton Roads, bringing her sons back from the war, and all eyes and hearts turned to the Pacific.

After the world's first atom bomb was dropped on Hiroshima on August 6, President Truman brought the news of victory again, this time of Japan's surrender, on August 14.

That night, a Virginian-Pilot reporter asked a sailor, "What are your postwar plans?" He grinned and answered, "I'm going to report in in about three more days—after I sober up."

It took several days for Norfolk and the nation to sober up, drunk on victory, and look ahead to the war's aftermath and an America changed forever.

A Cause for Celebration. After Victory in Europe Day (V-E Day) was celebrated May 8, 1945, as shown in this photo of downtown Norfolk, the nation held their breath for the war's end in Japan as well. That came August 14, when President Truman announced Japan's surrender. People tore up phone books to use as confetti, streets were jammed with honking cars and folks snake-dancing, and girls kissed every sailor they saw. (HRNM.)

VICTORY! Victory in Europe Day (V-E Day) is celebrated in this May 8, 1945 photo of Norfolk's Granby Street. In Norfolk, as in many other cities nationwide, the celebration came a bit prematurely. In *Conscripted City*, Marvin Schlegel writes: "On Saturday night, April 28, when a broadcast from San Francisco announced that news of the German surrender might be expected momentarily, Norfolk started to celebrate. The sky to the north was full of light and sound as Navy ships turned on their searchlights and blew their whistles. Restaurants and taverns closed up to get out of the way of the celebration. Auxiliary police called headquarters to ask for their instructions for handling the crowds. The staff in the Virginian-Pilot newsroom stood by, waiting for confirmation to get out an extra. Instead a half hour later came official word from President Truman that the report was without foundation." Not so a week later, Germany did surrender on May 7. Again the sirens, bells, and horns sounded as people gave thanks for victory in Europe and hoped for the same in the Pacific soon. (HRNM.)

BRING THE BOYS HOME. Since the majority of Norfolk's war efforts were in Europe, the region felt peace almost immediately after V-E Day, even before victory in Japan was won. By the end of June 1945, shiploads of soldiers and sailors began returning, some to be discharged, some to stay, and others to be redeployed. The military returned seized civilian property, like the Ford Motor Company in Berkley, the Nansemond Hotel in Ocean View, and the Cavalier Hotel in Virginia Beach. Problems arose, however; cities had become dependent on Shore Patrol to assist with policing and found themselves shortly without the extra help. Financially, Norfolk and the area became more independent, too, as government dollars that had been shared with municipalities dwindled or were cut off. Also, the region's infrastructure seemed to be dirty, broken, and worn-out from overuse during the war years. (OCGS.)

WAR OVER, GROWTH ON. When the war ended in 1945, as shown in this vintage photo, one in every ten Virginians lived in the Hampton Roads area; today it is about one in every five. Those numbers show the tremendous growth spurred by World War II and the continued military presence. The region has become less rural and more urban, less countrified and more cosmopolitan. (OCGS.)

A SPECIAL MEMORIAL DAY. This float from the naval air station goes down Norfolk's Granby Street in a Memorial Day parade on May 30, 1945, which was a very special occasion with the war in Europe. Everyone hoped things would soon get back to normal. However, for the time being, ration cards were still needed for sugar and gasoline, and the region was still overcrowded with extra military and civilian workers. (NPL.)

DOWN, BUT NOT OUT. Still nursing an assortment of ailments, patients at the Norfolk Naval Operating Base hospital respond to news of victory in Japan in this August 14, 1945 photo. The war had ended in Europe with Germany's surrender on May 7, 1945. Tens of thousands of war-wounded and war-weary soldiers and sailors were nursed back to health at the numerous military hospitals in Hampton Roads. (HRNM.)

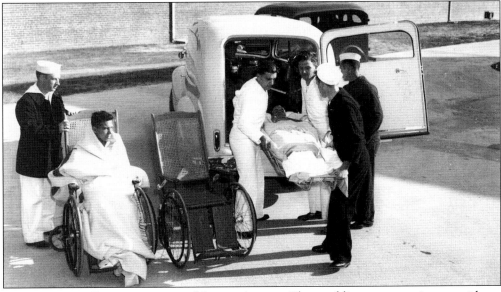

THE WOUNDED RETURNING FROM NORTH AFRICA. These soldiers are returning stateside on November 28, 1942, from operations in the North African invasion, Operation Torch. The November 8 offensive cost the Americans 837 wounded and 556 killed; many of the survivors also suffered from battle fatigue, or post-traumatic stress. The physically and psychologically injured returned to Portsmouth Naval Hospital (shown), Fort Story's United States Army Field Hospital, and other area medical centers. (NPL.)

PORTSMOUTH NAVAL HOSPITAL. This August 1944 photo shows patients at the Portsmouth Naval Hospital, the nation's oldest naval hospital. Building One opened in the 1830s. During World War II, as a German invasion of the East Coast seemed imminent, hospital facilities and staffing across Hampton Roads were beefed up, although by the end of the war, most services were for war-weary soldiers from European operations to convalesce. (NPL.)

TAKING CARE OF OUR OWN. By September 1944, Fort Story began transitioning to the role of convalescent hospital; the steady stream of wounded men coming from the European Theatre of Operations necessitated the expansion of hospital facilities (originally built in 1941). At the time of its closing on March 15, 1946, the hospital had accommodated more than 13,000 patients, at times hundreds more than the designated capacity of 1,800. (OCGS.)

DOING THEIR PART. Red Cross Gray Lady Mrs. Graham (Lorraine) Hinnant, the woman standing in the middle of this May 1945 photo, is shown with Lioness (Lions Club) Auxiliary members as they act as hostesses at the Red Cross Recreational Building at Fort Story. The other women are, at left, Mrs. H. Webb Brown and, at right, Mrs. Leo Hollenbeck; the soldiers are unidentified. Hinnant served with her mother at Fort Story for two years during the war as a recreational worker. The Gray Ladies would supervise parties, read books, and write letters on behalf of soldiers at the army hospital on base. Hinnant particularly worked in the convalescent hospital's psychiatric ward. "We got so many men after the Normandy Invasion," she said. "Some were totally paralyzed, not because there was anything physically wrong with them, but because of what they saw. They were shell shocked, or what we now call post traumatic stress. They saw so much killing." (OCGS.)

SURRENDER. Japan formally surrendered to Gen. Douglas MacArthur, representing the Allied forces, on September 2, 1945, aboard the USS *Missouri* (which had done its shakedown and battle practice in the Chesapeake Bay). MacArthur (January 26, 1880–April 5, 1964) was a brilliant, albeit egotistical, five-star U.S. Army general. He is buried in the MacArthur Memorial, established to honor his legacy, in downtown Norfolk, his mother's hometown. (OCGS.)

A CITY IN NEED. Not long after the ships unloaded on the piers at the Norfolk Naval Base (this vintage photo shows the USS *Missouri*, *Wisconsin*, *Franklin Delano Roosevelt*, and *Antietam*), the city realized the toll World War II took on its infrastructure. The *Virginian-Pilot* noted dirty and broken streets, shabby and rundown buildings, and other makeshift situations, concluding the war years had "literally pulled the city out of shape." (HRNM.)

Six

HAMPTON ROADS MILITARY
POSTWAR THROUGH TODAY

By the end of World War II, Americans turned their attention back to their own personal lives, hoping for an era of peace and prosperity. Service members returned to the States, and everyone hoped to get things back to normal.

For a while, the nation and the military relaxed, but it wouldn't last for long. In development of its own atomic weapons program, the Soviet Union successfully exploded a plutonium bomb on August 29, 1949, and the Cold War escalated. NATO's Allied Command Atlantic (ACLANT) would be headquartered in Norfolk in 1952.

The conflict in Korea escalated to an international struggle in June 1950. Although Congress had proposed to significantly reduce military spending that year, tensions with the Soviet Union and the war in Korea reversed its decision. The combined conflicts were the beginning of the postwar rearmament of the United States.

Then came Vietnam, increased tensions with the Soviets, and the first Gulf War. There has hardly been a downtime in the military, especially in Norfolk and the rest of Hampton Roads, except for a brief while in the 1990s. That would end with the terrorist attacks on September 11, 2001.

Today, the military presence in the region is bigger than ever, funneling tens of thousands through the area and billions of dollars into the economy.

YOU'RE IN THE ARMY NOW. In Newport News, Fort Eustis (*www.eustis.army.mil*) is the home of the U.S. Army Transportation Corps and the Transportation Corps Regiment, which includes the Transportation Center and School, the Aviation Logistics School, and the Non-commissioned Officer Academy. The fort employs around 9,600 military and 4,100 civilians. (OCGS.)

JOIN THE NAVY AND SEE THE WORLD. This 1950 photo shows a navy recruiting office in Norfolk. Although World War II was over, the military remained a popular avenue for young men and women who wanted to see the world and get assistance with their college education. There was a need for the recruits; by this time, tensions in Korea and the Cold War were escalating. (NPL.)

A NAVY TOWN. Since World War I, Norfolk and environs had established itself as a navy town. Soldiers and sailors, like those seen in this June 1953 photo crossing City Hall Avenue at Monticello Avenue in downtown Norfolk, were a common occurrence. The military presence also brings financial benefits to the region; Naval Air Station Oceana is the city of Virginia Beach's largest employer, with an annual payroll of more than $1 billion. (NPL.)

PULLING INTO PORT. The USS *Midway* arrives from a Mediterranean cruise in this March 1948 photo. There was little pause in military activity in Hampton Roads following World War II; the navy and other branches kept increasing their presence. Today, there are more than 200,000 military personnel and their family in the region. (NPL.)

FLYING HIGH. This 1950s photo shows the old control tower at Naval Air Station Oceana. The base continued to grow after World War II; by 1957, it was designated a Master Jet Base. Today Oceana (*www.nasoceana.navy.mil/*) is a complex of some 6,000 acres and home to more than 9,700 navy personnel conducting approximately 219,000 training operations each year. Eight F-14 Tomcat and 11 F/A-18 Hornet squadrons assigned to the Atlantic and Pacific Fleets are based here. (NASO.)

BOUNCING BACK. In October 2000, the guided missile destroyer USS *Cole* (DDG 67) was struck by terrorists in Yemen. Seventeen men and women lost their lives. Home-ported in Norfolk, the *Cole* (named for marine Sgt. Darrell Cole, who was killed at Iwo Jima during World War II) was repaired and returned to sea to fight in the war on terrorism. (U.S. Navy, Photographer's Mate 2c. Kevin Tidwell.)

SUBMARINE HEROES. Sailors on the Los Angeles–class attack sub USS *Minneapolis–Saint Paul* (SSN 708) moor the sub at Naval Station Norfolk (*www.navstanorva.navy/mil/*), the world's largest naval station, after a six-month deployment fighting the war on terrorism. There are 78 ships and 133 aircraft home-ported here; there are more than 3,100 ships' movements annually from one of the 14 piers on base. (U.S. Navy, Journalist Seaman Andy Zask.)

COMING HOME. Emotions run high for the 200,000-plus active duty military personnel and their family members as sailors and soldiers are shipped out and return home. The USO of Hampton Roads (*www.usohr.com*) works to enhance the quality of life of service members and their families through a number of services, including being shipside during deployments and homecomings with hot coffee, doughnuts, and a sympathetic ear. (U.S. Navy, Photographer's Mate Airman Orlando Quintero.)

COASTING ALONG. The U.S. Coast Guard cutter *Tampa* (WMEC 902) passes Fort Monroe on its way out to the Atlantic. The Fifth Coast Guard District (*www.uscg.mild/d5/*), located in Portsmouth, covers Coast Guard operations—including search and rescue, law enforcement, national security, environmental response, and aids to navigation—in Virginia, North Carolina, Maryland, Delaware, and parts of New Jersey and Pennsylvania. (U.S. Navy, Photographer's Mate 3c. Jason R. Zalasky.)

LIGHTING THE WAY. The Nimitz-class aircraft carrier USS *George Washington* (CVN 73) passes Cape Henry lights on Fort Story (*www.eustis.army.mil*/). The fort is a sub-installation of the U.S. Army Transportation Center and Fort Eustis, and it is the army's Logistics-Over-The-Shore (LOTS) training and test site. Also at the fort are U.S. Army Reserve units, U.S. Navy active and Reserve units, and a U.S. Marine Corp section. (U.S. Navy, Photographer's Mate 1c. Ken Riley.)

LANGLEY JETS OVER FORT MONROE. Since World War II, both Langley Air Force Base (the name changed from Langley Field in 1948) and Fort Monroe have grown exponentially. Langley AFB (*www.langley.af.mil*/) is the home of the First Fighter Wing and more than 10,000 service members and civilian workers. Since 1973, Fort Monroe (*www.monroe.army.mil*/) has been home to the Training and Doctrine Command (TRADOC) and has more than 2,000 military and civilian employees. (VASC.)

Seven

HOW TO CONTACT

Although World War II is a distant 60 years behind us, there are many ways to remember and honor the Greatest Generation today, especially in Hampton Roads. Across the region, there are a number of museums, monuments, and other venues dedicated in whole or in part to keeping the memory of the war alive.

Museums like the Old Coast Guard Station vividly display the hardships of the military and civilian population of the region with photographs and interactive exhibits. The Hampton Roads Naval Museum offers a wonderful look at the important role of the navy in the area, especially during World War II, and the adjacent USS Wisconsin affords a unique opportunity to step aboard a battleship from the era.

The rich history and lore of the World War II years in Hampton Roads has also been chronicled in a number of fine publications, with books like David Parker's History Next Door, *which shares 18 first-person stories from area veterans, and Al Chewning's* The Approaching Storm, *which paints a picture with words about the very real threat Norfolk and environs faced during the conflict.*

World War II is the war of our fathers, mothers, brothers, and sisters. It is the war of our grandparents. Remembering and honoring the heroes and victims of the Greatest Generation is a responsibility of all generations.

MEMORIAL WHERE FIRST ENGLISH COLONISTS LANDED AND NEW AND OLD LIGHTHOUSE, CAPE HENRY, VA.

HISTORIC FORT STORY. Although there are no tours of Fort Story, the army base is open for visitors to view the two Cape Henry lighthouses and the monument dedicated to the first landing of English settlers. Because it is an active military base, access to other areas of Fort Story is limited. Valid photo identification is required to enter the post. For more information, visit *www.apva.org/apva/cape_henry.php* or call 757-422-9421. (AJC.)

4A-H16

OLD COAST GUARD STATION MUSEUM. This historic Virginia Beach structure, built in 1903, was part of the U.S. Life Saving Service, later the U.S. Coast Guard, until it was decommissioned in 1969; it was later opened as a museum. There are two floors of exhibits. The lower gallery is the old boat room, and exhibits tell the story of the Life Saving Service. The upper gallery, where the surfmen would have slept, is dedicated to tales of Virginia shipwrecks and the Battle of the Atlantic in World War II. The exhibits about World War II are rich with local lore, chronicling the service the Coast Guard played in homeland security and the clear and present danger of German U-boats just off shore, as well as what the civilian population of Hampton Roads went through (rationing, blackouts, and the like) during the war years. A gift shop full of beach, lighthouse, and naval-themed merchandise, including local history books, is also on site. The Old Coast Guard Station is located at the Oceanfront on 24th Street. The phone number is 757-422-1587. The website is *www.oldcoastguardstation.com*. (OCGS.)

HAMPTON ROADS NAVAL MUSEUM AND THE USS WISCONSIN. Located within Nauticus, the National Maritime Center in downtown Norfolk, the Hampton Roads Naval Museum is one of 11 official navy museums, and it is dedicated to the study of 225 years of naval history in the Hampton Roads region. Colorful, informative, and educational exhibits include displays about all major military offensives (American Revolution through present day) involving the region, including the Battle of the Atlantic and World War II. The World War II exhibit includes artifacts from battles, newsreel films, and interactive displays that tell the story of the shipbuilding effort during the war, the German U-boats that operated off the coast, and the effect of the war on local life. Part of the museum is the World War II–era battleship USS *Wisconsin* (BB 64), which is open for touring. The ship, launched December 7, 1943, had a crew of 134 officers and 2,400 enlisted. Hampton Roads Naval Museum is located at 1 Waterside Drive. The phone number is 757-322-2987. The website is *www.hrnm.navy.mil/*. (PEH.)

TOP GUNS AT NAS OCEANA. Although not generally open to the public, Naval Air Station (NAS) Oceana and Naval Station Norfolk are open for tours seasonally through Hampton Roads Transit (HRT), the region's public transportation system. See page 125 for more information. (Photographer's Mate 1c. Matthew J. Thomas.)

MACARTHUR MEMORIAL. Located in Norfolk's restored 1850 city hall, the memorial traces the life and military career of Gen. Douglas MacArthur of the army and honors those who have served in the U.S. Armed Forces. Highlights include artifacts, photographs, documents, and memorabilia, as well as the general's trademark cap, sunglasses, and corncob pipe. The MacArthur Memorial is located at MacArthur Square on Bank Street in downtown Norfolk. The phone number is 757-441-2965. The website is *www.macarthurmemorial.org.* (PEH.)

124

PLACES TO VISIT

AIR POWER PARK AND MUSEUM. This park and museum has jets, missiles, rockets, and space artifacts in an outdoor display near Langley Air Force Base.
413 West Mercury Boulevard, Hampton
757-727-1163

CASEMATE MUSEUM ON FORT MONROE. The 1834 stone fort is within the active army base and chronicles the history of Fort Monroe and its artillery.
20 Bernard Road, Hampton
757-788-3391
www-tradoc.army.mil/museum/

FORT STORY. Although no tour of Fort Story is available, the base is accessible to view the Cape Henry lighthouses and first landing memorial cross. See page 121 for more information.

HAMPTON ROADS TRANSIT TOUR OF NAVAL STATION NORFOLK. The world's largest navy base is highlighted in a 45-minute tour, taking visitors dockside to the home of the Atlantic Fleet for a look at aircraft carriers, destroyers, submarines, and other U.S. Navy vessels. Tours run March through December and cost $7.50 for adults.
Naval Station Tour Center:
9079 Hampton Boulevard, Norfolk
757-222-6100
www.hrtransit.org/trllytour.html

HAMPTON ROADS TRANSIT TOUR OF NAS OCEANA. This tour of the world's largest Master Jet Base gives visitors a look at the more than 300 jet aircraft that call NAS Oceana home, including F-14 Tomcats and F/A-18 Hornets. Tours run June through September and cost $7.50 for adults.
Tourist kiosk:
Atlantic Avenue and Twenty-fourth Street, Virginia Beach
757-222-6100
www.hrtransit.org/trllytour.html

HAMPTON ROADS NAVAL MUSEUM AND THE USS WISCONSIN. See page 123 for more information.
1 Waterside Drive, Norfolk
757-322-2987
www.hrnm.navy.mil/

MACARTHUR MEMORIAL. See page 124 for more information.
Corner of Bank Street and City Hall Avenue, Norfolk
757-441-2965
www.macarthurmemorial.org

MARINERS' MUSEUM. This outstanding, massive collection recounts the maritime history of the region, including the permanent exhibit Defending the Seas.
100 Museum Drive, Newport News
757-596-2222
www.mariner.org

NAS OCEANA FLAME OF HOPE OBSERVATION PARK. Located on Oceana Boulevard about a half-mile from the base entrance, on the east side of the air station, this small park includes a POW/MIA memorial and an area to watch aircraft take off and land.

OLD COAST GUARD STATION. See page 122 for more information.
Twenty-fourth Street and Atlantic Avenue, Virginia Beach
757-422-1587
www.oldcoastguardstation.com

PORTSMOUTH NAVAL SHIPYARD MUSEUM. This museum chronicles the history of the nation's first drydock (1833), which is still in use today. The shipyard launched the first steel cruiser and battleship, and the first aircraft carrier was converted here as well.
2 High Street, Portsmouth
757-393-8591
www.portsnavalmuseums.com/

TOWN POINT PARK. Within Norfolk's Town Point park is the Norfolk Armed Services Memorial, which consists of 20 letters written home by soldiers in various conflicts, reproduced in bronze and scattered across the grass overlooking the Elizabeth River. Also featured is the *Homecoming* statue, a seven-foot cast bronze statue, which salutes the navy family with its depiction of a chief petty officer embracing his wife and son. Nearby, in Wisconsin Square, is *The Lone Sailor*, an exact replica of the famous statue at the Navy Memorial in Washington, D.C.

U.S. ARMY TRANSPORTATION MUSEUM ON FORT EUSTIS. Nearly 100 vehicles and aircraft, located both indoors and out, chronicle army transportation from the Revolution to the present day at this museum.
300 Washington Boulevard, Newport News
757-878-1115
www.eustis.army.mil/

VIRGINIA AIR & SPACE CENTER. The official visitor center for NASA Langley Research Center, the Virginia Air & Space Center holds more than 100 hands-on exhibits and full-sized aircraft floating in the 92-foot, glass-roofed atrium, highlighting the origins of flight and Hampton Roads role in aviation.
600 Settlers Landing Road, Hampton
757-727-0900
www.vasc.org

VIRGINIA WAR MUSEUM. The Virginia War Museum is home to a 50,000-item collection of military artifacts from 1775 through World War II and today.
9285 Warwick Boulevard, Newport News
757-247-8523
www.warmuseum.org

RECOMMENDED READING

Chewning, Alpheus J. *The Approaching Storm: U-Boats off the Virginia Coast During World War II*. Richmond, VA: Brandylane Publishers, 1994.

Morison, Samuel Eliot and Dudley Wright Knox. *The Battle of the Atlantic: September 1939–May 1943*. Urbana, IL: University of Illinois Press, 2001.

Parker, David. *History Next Door: Stories of World War II by Hampton Roads Veterans*. Pittsburgh: Dorrance Publishing, 2001.

Powell, James R. and Dr. Alan B. Flanders. *Wolf at the Door: The World War II Antisubmarine Battle for Hampton Roads*. Richmond, VA: Brandylane Publishers, 2003.

Schlegel, Marvin W. *Conscripted City: Norfolk in World War II*. Norfolk: Norfolk War History Commission, 1951.

Tazewell, William L. *Norfolk's Waters: An Illustrated Maritime History of Hampton Roads*. Woodland Hills, CA: Windsor Publications, 1982.

Yarsinske, Amy Waters. *Mud Flats to Master Jet Base: Fifty Years at NAS Oceana*. Gloucester Point, VA: Hallmark Publishing, 2001.

HEARING THE VOICES OF WAR. Almost every person alive in the 1940s had his or her own story to tell about World War II. Marine Cpl. John William Evans, the author's grandfather, pictured here, was no different. Enlisting on May 1, 1943, he stormed the beaches at Iwo Jima and was a witness to the famous flag-raising on Mount Suribachi. Later, after the atomic bomb was dropped on Hiroshima, he was assigned there for a time during the Occupation of Japan, amid the blast aftermath. He was honorably discharged January 12, 1946. His stories were as vivid as any movie, but sadly, many were not written down until after his death in 1985. That first-hand, living history continues to die—most surviving vets are now between the ages of 75 and 85, and it is estimated more than 1,000 of them pass away each day. The Veterans History Project seeks to preserve those stories by chronicling and categorizing recollections from the Greatest Generation. For more information, contact the Library of Congress's American Folklife Center at 888-371-5848 or online, at *www.loc.gov/folklife/vets*. (PEH.)

ABOUT THE AUTHOR

ABOUT THE AUTHOR. Patrick Evans-Hylton was raised by his grandparents and in his childhood was fascinated by the many stories of World War II told by his grandfather, Bill Evans, a marine veteran who served in the Pacific from 1943 through 1946. Patrick also considers himself a local historian and especially loves the rich military history found in his adopted southeastern Virginia. He is also the author of *The Suffolk Peanut Festival* and *Smithfield: Ham Capital of the World*. Patrick, a freelance writer (www.evanshyltonink.com) has written for several area publications and is an editor at *Hampton Roads Magazine*, a regional city and lifestyle magazine. He also is co-host of "The Restaurant Show," reporting on food and the culinary scene in Hampton Roads, which airs Thursday nights from 6 to 8 p.m. on WTAR 850 AM. (PEH.)

BIBLIOGRAPHY

In addition to the publications referenced in the "Recommended Reading" section of chapter seven, the following resources were used in the research of this book.

Hampton Roads Naval Museum Website, August–November 2004. <http://www.hrnm.navy.mil/>

United States Air Force Website, August–November 2004.

United States Army Website, August–November 2004. <http://www.army.mil/>

United States Coast Guard Website, August–November 2004. <http://www.uscg.mil/>

United States Navy Website, August–November 2004. <http://www.navy.mil/>